STARR ROXANNE HILTZ

CREATING COMMUNITY SERVICES FOR WIDOWS
A Pilot Project

National University Publications
KENNIKAT PRESS   //   1977
Port Washington, N. Y.   //   London

Manufactured in the United States of America

Published by
Kennikat Press Corp.
Port Washington, N. Y./London

Library of Congress Cataloging in Publication Data

Hiltz, Starr Roxanne.
    Creating community services for widows.

    (National university publications)
    Bibliography: p.
    Includes index.
    1. Widows—United States. 2. Social work with widows—
United States. I. Title.
HQ1058.5.U5H54   362.8   76-18292
ISBN 0-8046-9157-6

FOR MY PARENTS

CONTENTS

LIST OF TABLES AND FIGURES

PREFACE

This is an account of a new kind of social service, a center where widows may come for professional help with their emotional, financial, and legal problems, and where they may socialize with other widows and begin to take steps to rebuild their lives. The data on which it is based are the result of a formal evaluation of the pilot project phase of the Widows Consultation Center. The account is designed as a kind of handbook to make the experience of the Widows Consultation Center available to those who are interested in trying to improve services for widows in their community.

During its first three years of operation, the Center was sponsored by the Prudential Insurance Company of America as a community service. The Prudential also financed the evaluation research effort for three years. After this pilot project phase, the funding of the Widows Consultation Center and the specifics of the services it offers underwent numerous changes. No data on these subsequent developments are included here; this book is a "slice of history" which describes only the pilot project. Subsequent to the writing of this book, the Center closed in January, 1976 due to problems in obtaining adequate funding. The data on clients and their reactions to the Center are drawn from the case histories and follow-up interviews for the widows who came to the Center during its first eighteen months.

The Prudential executive who was involved at all stages of the planning for the Center itself and for the evaluation research on which this book draws heavily is Martin Albaum, Director of Research. I am grateful to him for extensive comments on earlier drafts of the manuscript. This is not to imply that this report necessarily reflects the opinions of Dr. Albaum or of the Prudential.

I am also indebted to the staff and officers of the Widows Consultation

Center for their generosity in spending many days answering my questions about the operation of the Center during the period when the research was conducted. However, it should be noted at the outset that the officers did not favor the publication of the full study. They felt that some of the information about the Center's operations which is included here is "private"; when they gave it to me and I recorded it on my tape recorder or note pad, they did not realize that I meant to publish it. Secondly, they felt that the changes in programs which have been instituted since the research was completed have solved some of the problems that existed during the pilot stage and which are documented here.

I would also like to thank the excellent and dedicated women who conducted the follow-up interviews with clients: Judith Pekowsky, Esther Wallach, and Doris Meritz. And, of course, this study would not have been possible without the cooperation of the over two hundred and fifty widows who spent about an hour each sharing their experiences as a widow and their opinions about the Center. Other persons who have been very generous in contributing materials include Diane DeGraves, Director of the Widows Consultation Centre in Winnipeg, and Dr. Robert Weiss of the Harvard Medical School Bereavement Project.

On the level of personal support, I would like to thank Dean Dorothy Schneider of Upsala College for encouraging me to have this study published, and the always-patient mother-substitute who presided over my children's needs while I was working on this manuscript, Marjorie Fischer. My husband, George, contributed editorial and emotional support and typed the entire manuscript. Finally, I would like to thank my parents, Mildred and John Smyers, for socializing me to believe that I could be anything I want to be—even an author! I hope that my readers will not feel that they were terribly mistaken.

CREATING COMMUNITY SERVICES FOR WIDOWS

THE AUTHOR

Dr. Hiltz spent the better part of five years on the research and analysis which went into this book. *Creating Community Services for Widows: A Pilot Project* represents the evaluation of the work of the Widow's Consultation Center of New York City which had been funded by the Prudential Insurance Company for whom she acted as a consultant. Dr. Hiltz (Ph. D. Columbia University) usually spends her time chairing the Department of Sociology and Anthropology at Upsala College in New Jersey but during the academic year 1976–1977 she was appointed a Visiting Fellow in the Sociology Department at Princeton University. Very much a feminist, she is active in the women's movement and conducts seminars on sex roles.

WIDOWHOOD AS A NEGLECTED SOCIAL PROBLEM

The death of a spouse is one of the most serious life crises which a person can face. There is the immediate emotional crisis of bereavement, which, if not fully worked through, may result in permanent symptoms of mental disorder. In addition, there is generally a need for a total restructuring of the widow's life, as she finds herself much poorer, socially isolated, and left without a meaningful life pattern.

Widowhood is shared by a very large number of women: in 1974, there were 9,814,000 widows in the United States, and their numbers have been increasing by about 100,000 a year (Bureau of the Census, 1974). This is about 13% of all women over the age of eighteen. Growth in potential clients for services to widows is sure to continue for the rest of this century, since Bureau of the Census projections (1972) indicate an increase of 43% in the size of the total population over sixty-five by the year 2000.

The genesis of widowhood as a social problem in America can be traced to the joint operation of demographic changes and the persistence of a set of values defining a woman mainly in terms of her role as a wife. American women have a longer life expectancy than American men, by about seven years at the present time. Demographically, it would make sense for women to marry younger males, but the norms and opportunities are such that the initial mortality differences are compounded by the tendency to marry older men. Since only about one American woman out of twenty never marries at all, the inevitable result is that larger and larger proportions of women become and remain widows (see Table 1.1)

Most preindustrial societies have very clear roles for widows to play. For example, in traditional Indian society, a Brahmin widow was supposed to commit suttee by throwing herself on her husband's funeral pyre; if she did not, she was condemned to live out her life dressed in a single coarse garment, with shaven head, eating only one meal a day, and shunned by others as "unlucky." Another extreme solution, practiced in many African societies, was automatic remarriage: the wife and children were "inherited" by a younger brother of the deceased or other heir, and the widow became one of his wives in a polygamous family. (See Lopata, 1972, for further descriptions of these customs and those of many other societies in regard to widows.) Even if such prescribed actions and roles were not particularly desirable from the widow's point of view, at least it was clear exactly what she was to do with the rest of her life.

Table 1.1

WIDOWS IN THE UNITED STATES, 1974

Age Group	% Widows
20-29	0.4
30-39	1.3
40-54	6.4
55-64	20.5
65-74	42.6
75+	68.2

Source: Bureau of Census, 1974.

The new widow in America and other Western, industrialized societies, has lost not only a husband, but her own main functions, reason for being, and self-identity. In spite of the emergence of "women's liberation," most women who are becoming widows today have defined themselves primarily as wives and mothers. Helena Znanieki Lopata sums up the situation in *Widowhood in an American City,* a study of Chicago widows:

In spite of the rapid industrialization, urbanization, and increasing complexity of the social structure of American society, the basic cluster of social roles available to, and chosen by, its women has been that of wife-mother-housewife. This fact imposes some serious problems upon the last stage of their lives, similar to the problems of retirement in the lives of men who had concentrated upon their occupational roles. The wife-mother-housewife often finds herself with children who are grown, absent from her home, and independent of her as a basic part of their lives; her husband has died, and her household no longer contains a client segment. The traditional woman had been involved, at least in myth (see Shanas, 1968), in a three generational family circle, surrounded ideally with her husband's family of orientation and her own family of procreation. The absence of her husband would be less dramatic under circumstances of an extended kinship group than when he is the only other member of a working, living, and companionate team (Lopata, 1973, pp. 87-88).

Lynn Caine, in her poignant account of her own bereavement and eventual readjustment with professional help, has written a most moving description of the effects of the wrenching away of one's main social and self-identity that occurs with the death of a husband:

"Widow" is a harsh and hurtful word. It comes from the Sanskrit and means "empty". . .

After my husband died, I felt like one of those spiraled shells washed up on the beach. Poke a straw through the twisting tunnel, around and around, and there is nothing there. No flesh. No life. Whatever lived there is dried up and gone.

Our society is set up so that most women lose their identities when their husbands die. Marriage is a symbiotic relationship for most of us. We draw our identities from our husbands. We add ourselves to our men, pour ourselves into them and their lives. We exist in their reflection. And then. . .? If they die. . .? What is left? It's wrenching enough to lose the man who is your lover, your companion, your best friend, the father of your children, without losing yourself as well (Caine, 1974, pp. 181 and 1).

It should be noted that Caine had a fine job for many years before her husband died, but that this did not alleviate the necessity and pain of totally restructuring her social roles.

Three quarters of all wives will become widows. The median age for the onset of widowhood is about fifty-six, and a woman widowed at that age can expect to live about twenty more years. "Of the widows bereft of their spouse at age 65, somewhat more than half can expect to live 15 years or longer, and about a third still have 20 years of life before them" (Metropolitan Life Insurance Company, 1962, pp. 1-4). Remarriage is not a likely solution: there are fewer than two million widowers in the United States (one for every five widows), and they are likely to marry younger women.

As Lopata points out (1973, p. 17), "Life styles for American widows are generally built upon the assumption that they are young and can soon remarry or that they are very old and removed from the realm of actual involvement. The trouble is that most widows are neither, but the society has not taken sufficient cognizance of this fact to modify the facilities and roles available to them." A woman is likely to spend as much time as a widow as she does raising children. Although she was socialized all through her early life for the wife-and-motherhood role, she typically has had no preparation at all for the widowhood role. The whole subject has been taboo, and few women prepare ahead of time for this statistically probable status.

Despite the statistical facts and personal tragedies that make widowhood a major social problem, it has been until recently an almost totally "neglected aspect of the family life cycle" both in terms of sociological research and of public and private social resources dealing with it, even though it is "a pervasive social problem directly encompassing increasing numbers of women and their families and indirectly affecting many others" (Berardo, 1968, p. 200). One study of such family strains, focusing on the effect of having a widowed mother upon middle-class males, found that perceived obligations of son to mother and one-way aid are a dominant pattern. This typically results in loss of affection and resentment of her dependent status on the part of the son (Adams, 1969). The problems of readjustment faced by widows are not only individual tragedies, but also a great societal waste, since without help, many widows live out their lives in bitterness and dependence rather than as contributing, happy members of our society. The social service community must expand the availability of programs for widows, given the scale and the seriousness of the problem involved.

Many existing organizations, such as family service and mental health agencies or the growing number of women's centers, may feel that the problems of widows can be dealt with without any new or special programs. However, the current system of services has not been effective either in motivating troubled widows to come for help or in identifying specific requests by clients who are widows as one part of a general bereavement and readjustment problem. For instance, Silverman (1966) screened the intake of the seven agencies in the Boston area most likely to have widowed clients, including Family Service, the Community Child Guidance Clinic, and the Community Adult Psychiatric Clinic. Over a four-month period, the family agencies received no applications from widows. There were four applications for homemaker service, but "the agencies did not associate the call for help with the bereavement" (p. 180). There were nine calls for psychiatric services from bereaved persons. Reviewing the nature of the requests and diagnoses (depression, alcoholism, schizophrenia), Silverman concludes that "We get an appreciation of how complex the bereaved's problems are and that psychiatric services only briefly touch one aspect of them" (p. 181). To make widows feel that they have a place to go where they can receive understanding and help, it is necessary to develop and publicize a program as being specifically for widows and to design the program to deal with most of the problems the widow is likely to have without relying on referrals to outside agencies.

I will describe what was learned from the evaluation research on a pilot social service project for widows about their problems and what can be done to aid and counsel the widow. The agency is the Widows Consultation Center in New York City, established in 1969. That it should have been the *first* professional social work agency in the United States devoted to the problems of widows is a comment upon the cultural tendency to avoid anything that has to do with death. The data are based on case histories compiled by the social workers, follow-up interviews with the clients, unstructured interviews with the staff, and tape recordings of group therapy sessions. Before turning to the nature and results of this pilot project, however, we shall briefly review what is generally known about bereavement and widowhood and the previous attempts by social agencies in the United States and abroad to provide services to widows.

BEREAVEMENT AS A KIND OF ILLNESS

As we have seen, widowhood represents a social problem in the sense that the operation of demographic forces and social norms has created millions of widows who are likely to be poverty-stricken, socially isolated, left without a meaningful life pattern or social function, and psychologically or emotionally troubled. In their struggle to find a new life for themselves, they encounter both ageism and sexism. That they are a high-risk group in terms of psychological pathology has been recognized from the beginning of social research. For instance, in 1897 Emile Durkheim pointed out the relatively high suicide rates of widows and commented:

The suicides occurring at the crisis of widowhood . . . are really due to domestic anomy resulting from the death of the husband or wife. A family catastrophe occurs which affects the survivor. He is not adapted to the new situation in which he finds himself and accordingly offers less resistance to suicide (Durkheim, 1951, p. 259).

The problems of widowhood can be analytically separated into two kinds. First, there are the emotional and psychological traumas of grief and mourning, of finally letting go of one's old emotional ties and roles, which centered on the husband. If this working through of grief is successfully accomplished, the widow is in a position to face a second set of problems, having to do with building a new life, a new set of role relationships, and a new identity.

Much of the psychological literature on grief represents an elaboration of Freud's theories. For Freud, grief (or grief works) is the process by which bereaved persons struggle to disengage the loved object. There is a kind of emotional bond fused with energy that is bound up in memories and ideas related to former interactions with the loved person. The mourner has to spend a great deal of time and effort in bringing to consciousness all of these memories in order to gradually set free the energy, to break the tie (Freud, 1917).

A very influential study of "normal" bereavement by Lindemann in 1944 established the concept that normal bereavement consists of a number of stages:

1. Numbness and disbelief, a tendency to deny the death, not to accept the fact that "he is *really* dead, gone forever." This numbness often extends through all the funeral proceedings and lasts for several weeks.

2. This is followed by a period of strong emotion. There is usually crying, which may be accompanied by psychosomatic symptoms (headache, insomnia); feelings of guilt—("If I had done so-and-so, maybe he wouldn't have died"); anger—("Why me! It is so unfair!"); hostility and blame—("The doctors killed him."); often preoccupation with memories of the deceased and an idealization of him.

3. Incapacitating feelings of sadness and loneliness, depression, loss of customary patterns of conduct and of motivation to try to go on living. This may be followed by a recovery phase.

At one time grief—as in the extended "pining away" of the third stage—was recognized as a cause of death and listed on death certificates. As Glick et al. (1974) have concluded from their extensive studies of bereavement, "the death of a spouse typically gives rise to a reaction whose duration must be measured in years rather than in weeks" (p. 10).

A recent review of some of the hundreds of books and articles on death and bereavement summarizes the variety of "morbid" or abnormal grief reactions that may occur, especially when the mourner does not express emotion or refuses to deal with the loss. These include delay of the grief reactions for months or even years; overactivity without a sense of loss; irritability and hostility toward others continuing indefinitely; acquisition of the physical symptoms of the deceased's last illness, or of other psychosomatically based illnesses such as ulcerative colitis; and such intense depression and feelings of worthlessness that suicide is attempted (VanCoevering, 1971, p. 6).

In his recent book, *Bereavement,* Parkes constructed a concise summary of the incidence of some common aspects of grief from five studies of young and middle-aged widows (see Table 1.2). These are by no means representative samples of all widows, but the figures show the almost universal occurrence of many serious emotional problems among the bereaved.

FINANCIAL PROBLEMS

When we move from the trauma and desolation of grief to the subsequent life-changes and problems faced by the widow we see that widowhood is very much a sex role for which there is no comparable male role. As Glick et al. (1974, p. 262) summarize the differences between their samples of widows and of widowers, "Insofar as the men reacted simply to the *loss of a loved other*, their responses were *similar* to those of widows, but insofar

Table 1.2
Percentage of Widows Showing Common Aspects of Grief
(Based on Five Previous Studies of Widows)

Aspects of grief	Hobson (1964) Unselected U. K. widows age < 60 N = 40 %	Yamiamoto et al. (1969) Japanese motor accident widows age < 55 N = 20 %	Marris (1958) Unselected U. K. widows age < 60 N = 72 %	Parkes (1971) London study Unselected U. K. widows age < 65 N = 22 %	Parkes (1969) Bereaved psychiatric patients (women) age < 60 N = 14 %
Depression/anxiety	——	85	100	85	100
Apathy	73	55	61	——	50
Insomnia	88	70	79	45	71
Sense of presence of the deceased	80	90	50	55	50
Difficulty in accepting face of loss	50	60	23	59	79

Source: Parkes, 1972, p. 211.

as men reacted to the *traumatic disruption of their lives*, their responses were *different*." Perhaps this differential impact is strongest in terms of the financial impact of the death, because for the widow, it almost always means the loss of the main source of financial support for the family and a drastic lowering of the standard of living which they can afford.

The most complete data about the financial condition of widows comes from a survey of a sample of 1,744 widows whose husbands had died in 1966, conducted by the Life Insurance Agency Management Association in 1968-69 and published in 1970. Of course, this underrepresents the older, long-term widows who would be especially likely to be poor. They found that for 28%, there was at least a year between the onset of the final illness or disability and the death. This is a financially and emotionally draining experience. Only two thirds of widows with medical bills received any health insurance payments, and for them the health insurance paid an average of 77% of the bill. Mean final expenses were $3,600, with life and health insurance combined covering only 64% of the final expenses. For the remainder, the widows had to deplete savings or use income from their social security or earnings, etc.

The average per capita monthly income payments of the widows from all sources was only $155. Thirty-two percent of the widows reported that they had trouble managing their finances.

By two to three years after the onset of widowhood, the incomes of the widows' families were down an average of 44% from previous levels, and 58% had incomes that fell below the amount that would have been necessary to maintain their family's former standard of living. This is despite the fact that among those who had had any proceeds from life insurance left after final expenses, 44% had used up part of this for living expenses, and 14% had already used it all.

In Lopata's sample of Chicago widows, 60% had annual family incomes of under $3,000. Compared with data on family income when the husband was alive, widows' incomes have dropped precipitously. As she points out, "regardless of the past, the present income situation of the widow is generally bad, falling below the poverty line" (Lopata, 1973, p. 37).

FINDING NEW SOCIAL ROLES

Before widowhood, a married woman relates to most other people in terms of her status as somebody's wife. Most of her role relationships will have to be adjusted or perhaps terminated, and she will have to establish new relationships and roles if her life is to be a satisfying one. The difficulties an older woman in our society is likely to encounter in establishing such a new set of role relationships are reflected by the fact that Lopata found half of the widows she studied considered loneliness their greatest problem and another third listed it second. Another measure of the tendency towards social isolation of widows is that 58% agreed with the statement, "One problem of being a widow is feeling like a 'fifth wheel'" (Lopata, 1972, pp. 91 and 346).

Lopata's work focuses on the widow's role relationships in regard to motherhood, kin relationships, friendship, and community involvement, including employment. Among her findings are that "women who develop satisfactory friendships, who weather the transition period and solve its problems creatively, tend to have a higher education, a comfortable income, and the physical and psychic energy needed to initiate change" (p. 216). In other words, they are not the average widow, who is likely to have a high school education or less, low income, depleted physical energy due to advancing age, and depleted psychic energy due to the trauma of bereavement and its associated problems.

In trying to establish a social identity, the widow comes face to face with her stigmatized status in our society, her "spoiled identity" from the point of view of her former friends. As Parkes points out in *Bereavement,* this stigma is always an important factor in adjustment to bereavement:

By stigma I mean the change in attitude that takes place in society when a person dies. Every widow discovers that people who were previously friendly and approachable become embarrassed and strained in her presence. Expressions of sympathy often have a hollow ring and offers of help are not followed up. It often happens that only those who share the grief or have themselves suffered a major loss remain at hand. It is as if the widow has become tainted with death in much the same way as the funeral director (Parkes, 1972, p. 8).

OTHER PROGRAMS THAT AID WIDOWS

If the problems of widowhood are serious and widely experienced, then what kinds of community services exist to help? Perhaps surprisingly, to our knowledge there has never before been a professional social work agency in the United States devoted exclusively to widows and accepting all widowed people, regardless of religion, age, and specific community of residence. There have been some other programs to help widows, however, and these are briefly described below.

"CRUSE: The Organization for Widows and Their Children" was established in Britain in 1959 and built up a large number of local clubs throughout the United Kingdom and in New Zealand. "We are primarily a group of friends working for families, often similar to our own, who have encountered difficulties of all kinds through the death of the breadwinner," states its annual report. At the end of the first ten years, its program included a monthly newsletter for members, personal contact schemes to alleviate loneliness, social groups in twenty-five areas, and many publications and fact sheets on problems of widows (Annual Report, 1967-68).

The "Widow-to-Widow Program" was a project set up by Harvard University's Laboratory of Community Psychiatry, with the program itself directed by Phyllis Silverman, a Ph. D. in social work. It was funded for a limited time only. In studying the services which might be offered to widows, Dr. Silverman felt that self-help groups in which widows offered aid to one another might be most useful. As she explains in an unpublished paper:

The Widow-to-Widow Program was an experiment to test the feasibility of another widow becoming a caregiver to the newly widowed. It was hypothesized that she would be able to use her own experience to help others, that her special empathy would enable her to understand the support needed, that she could accept the new widow's distress over an extended period of time, and that she would be accepted if she offered her assistance to the new widow.

The target population was defined as all widows under sixty in a sub-community of Boston, with the names gotten from death certificates. Five widows were originally recruited as aides, chosen as having personal skills in dealing with people and as representatives of the dominant racial and religious groups in the community. The aide wrote the new widow a letter saying that she would call on her at a particular time and day at least three weeks after the death, unless the widow telephoned and requested her not to visit. Of the ninety-one widows located in the first seven months of the program, sixty-four accepted contact, half by visit and half by telephone. (Later figures showed an overall acceptance rate of 60%.) The aides offered friendship as well as advice and assistance with specific problems. In addition, group discussion meetings and social events such as a cook-out were organized, to which all of the widows were invited (Silverman, 1969, pp. 333-37).

As Silverman describes the role of the aide (1972, pp. 100-101), it was similar to that later played by the discussion group leader or social caseworker at the Widows Consultation Center:

The aide was comfortable talking about grief and the difficulties in accommodating to it. . . She was able to listen, to be empathetic, and to understand the turmoil of grief. She was not upset by tears, nor distressed by the length of time it could take for a widow to find a new direction but she could get annoyed and push a little when she knew it was time to take hold and try something new. . . The aide encourages, prods, insists, and sometimes even takes the widow by the hand and goes through the motions with her.

Subsequent to the demise of the Widow-to-Widow Program, sociologist Robert Weiss and his colleagues at the Laboratory of Community Psychiatry began developing a program of eight "seminars" for the bereaved. Each of eight weekly meetings begins with a lecture of about forty-five minutes on some aspect of bereavement. After each lecture, small discussion groups are formed, which meet for about an hour and a half with a staff member as leader, during which they might discuss the subject of the lecture or take any other direction the members of the group desire. There is a wine and cheese party at the last meeting, and then a "reunion" of the group about six weeks after the last meeting (Weiss, 1975, and personal communication).

In April 1972, the Widows Consultation Center proudly spawned its first "offspring." Also called the Widows Consultation Centre, it was set up as a part of the services of the YWCA in Winnipeg and financed by a three-year pilot program grant by the Great West Life Assurance Company. Occasional references will be made to some of the ways in which the Canadian Centre's experiences have differed from those of the New York Center, particularly in the final chapter on comparative costs of various types of services to widows. (See unpublished reports by Diane DeGraves, director of the Canadian Centre, for more information.)

Certainly this short list of social service organizations aimed at widows points out an unfilled need for help for widows in our society. (For a list of other organizations offering services to widows, see Appendix A.)

WHY A WIDOWS CONSULTATION CENTER: AN EXAMPLE WHICH SUMMARIZES THE NEED

Why should there be a need for a formal community agency, staffed by professionals, to deal with a problem such as widowhood? Isn't this the kind of personal crisis that is best handled by oneself, one's family, and friends?

One way of gaining insight into the need for an institutional source of aid and support for widows is to look at one of the problems that widows bring to the Center and to explore its nature and the reasons why informal sources are often inadequate for dealing with the problem. Let us use the example of loneliness.

Loneliness is one of the most pervasive and long-term problems reported by widows. References to it occur again and again as one looks through the case histories and follow-up interviews collected from the widows who came to the Center. Some examples of these comments are: "I was all alone and was at a loss about what to do with myself . . . " "The loss and emptiness felt when one loses a dear one is not easily filled . . . " "I was very lonely. One day I was a wife, the next day I was nothing . . . "

As Lopata points out, *loneliness* is a word used to describe many different aspects of feelings related to a subjectively inadequate frequency and/or depth of interaction with others (Lopata, 1969). Among the various aspects of loneliness are missing the deceased husband as a specific, unique person and companion with whom one shared experiences; curtailment of couple-based social activities and relationships which require a male escort; and loneliness as deprivation of the style of life, daily routines, and leisure activities which the couple enjoyed.

The solution to loneliness involves the successful development of new roles, relationships, and activities. As Lopata states, "Somewhere during the grief period these various forms of loneliness seem to combine into a very strong mood of depression. Efforts of relatives and friends, initiative behavior by the widow itself, or a combination of these gradually lead to solutions of some of the problems, to 'grief work'. . . which rebuilds the life around new relations."

Not all widows have relatives or friends who are willing or able to help them in their grief work and rebuilding, however, or who have the background and personality to take the necessary initiative without advice and support. This is especially true given the following factors:

1. Death and grief are taboo subjects in our society. Even close friends and relatives are likely to try to avoid discussing the widow's feelings about her husband after a short period.

2. Many friends are no longer available, because the relationship was couple-based. The widow feels like a "fifth wheel" if she tries to continue these relationships.

3. Given the nuclear family structure and widespread geographic mobility of American society, many widows have few relatives nearby, or else these relatives feel that their duty has been discharged by simply participating in the funeral ceremonies.

4. Many women have been taught by our society to be extremely passive and dependent on their husbands. They lack the necessary self-confidence and experience to take major steps to reorganize their lives on their own.

The services offered by the Center can be viewed as substitute or supplementary sources of support for dispelling loneliness and grief and building new relationships, for that large proportion of widows in our society who lack the personal and social resources necessary to accomplish these tasks on their own. Weiss (1974, p. 214) refers to organizations such as the Widows Consultation Center as providing a kind of "supplementary community" which can be compared in this respect to the kinds of needs that Parents Without Partners meets for the recently divorced. Loneliness is a kind of "deficit" situation which can be met by the supplementary community:

The organization seemed to respond in its programming to four types of deficit: (a) the absence of a sustaining community; (b) the absence of friends in similar situations; (c) the absence of support for a sense of worth; and (d) the absence of emotional attachment. Its response to each of these deficits took the form of making available appropriate supplementary relationships (Weiss, 1974, p. 214).

Another way of conceptualizing the role played by an organization such as the Widows Consultation Center and of finding parallels in other kinds of services is in terms of "preventive" psychiatry or social work intervention at a point of personal crisis. A British study (Maddison, 1968, pp. 223-33) described the need in these terms:

Conjugal bereavement is seen to be one example of a crisis which may have far-reaching consequences in terms of physical and/or mental ill health. The research reported here suggests that widows at high risk of an unsatisfactory outcome may be able to be identified shortly after bereavement. One factor of outstanding importance in this regard appears to be the widow's perception that the persons in her environment are failing to meet her needs, or are actively blocking the expression of affect . . . The degree and quality of the support which is available to the widow during crisis is of importance in its own right in determining the manner in which the crisis is resolved.

The needs which widows have for a professional source of support can be met not only by setting up a special agency for widows. Given the costs involved, a specialized agency is impractical for all but the largest communities. However, the needs of widows can also be met by developing special services which reach out to widows *within* broader purpose organizations, such as family counselling agencies, programs for senior citizens, and women's centers. In developing such services and programs for widows, it is hoped that social service workers may draw upon the experiences of the Widows Consultation Center, which are reported in the chapters which follow.

2

THE PILOT PROJECT OF THE WIDOWS CONSULTATION CENTER

This chapter will give a brief chronological account of the development of the Widows Consultation Center during its three years as a pilot social service project dedicated to the development of information and advisory services to aid widows. Subsequent sections will treat most of the aspects discussed in much more detail.

In 1965 Martin Albaum, Director of Research at the Prudential Insurance Company, did a study of life insurance beneficiaries, based on lengthy interviews with one hundred widows. Among the key findings, according to Dr. Albaum was

the discovery that many widows wanted some source of advice on the financial, legal, child raising, housing, job hunting, and social problems that widowhood had brought them. We thought seriously about how Prudential could meet this need within its own organization. We came to the conclusion that we did not have the expertise to deal with most of these problems. Where we did have some expert knowledge, such as in the financial field, we did not want either to assume the liability of giving advice or to raise the suspicion that we were giving self serving advice.

The need of widows for help beyond the financial aid of an insurance check remained unfulfilled until late in 1968. At that time, two New York women prominent in social service who had become concerned about the lack of organized sources of help for widows heard of Albaum's study and approached him with a proposal that Prudential fund a pilot social service agency to give advice to widows. The founders, the author (who was a Prudential employee at the time), and Dr. Albaum prepared a formal proposal with supporting materials and a research design. These were presented to the Prudential Board with a request for a large grant, not to exceed

$400,000, to fund a three-year pilot project and research on it.

Prudential agreed to fund the Widows Consultation Center for the three-year pilot period. The interest of the Prudential fell into three areas:

1. To obtain more information about the problems of widows. It was hoped that this new body of information could be used to help Prudential improve its services to widows.

2. Evaluation of the effectiveness of the pilot project. It was agreed that this required that the evaluator have access to all case records and to group discussion sessions with due regard for preserving the anonymity of clients. The purpose of the evaluation research was to document the services developed and the extent to which they met existing needs, in order to facilitate the possible establishment of similar services in other communities.

3. A way for the Prudential Insurance Company of America to concretely demonstrate its responsibility as a "corporate citizen."

Arrangements were made that the grant would be paid in quarterly installments, authorized regularly by Albaum as long as he was satisfied that the Center was adhering to the agreement.

These initial negotiations took over a year, and the founders of the Center were immediately faced with the first of a series of financial squeezes: rising rents and other costs associated with inflation forced them to curtail some plans in order to live within the budget.

The first concrete problem encountered was finding a usable space in Manhattan, in a "safe" neighborhood and at a bearable price. The director, a caseworker, and a secretary were temporarily housed in a Prudential agency in Manhattan while the search was conducted. They hoped to find seven or eight large rooms in a residential building, which would include kitchen facilities and be open weekends and evenings. Nothing could be located after several weeks of searching, however, so the founders settled on a modern but rather small office suite of six rooms plus a reception area in an office building. It had no running water or a bathroom of its own, let alone a kitchen. The cramped and businesslike quarters had the unfortunate result of limiting the expansion of the services beyond what could be provided by three caseworkers and the director and of discouraging evening and weekend activities on the premises, since the building was dark and empty then. This scarcity of suitable space was a local and temporary problem and probably would not represent such a stumbling block for other services.

The Widows Consultation Center was ready for clients in July 1970. The fact that over a year had elapsed between conception of the idea and delivery of the services was perhaps the first lesson that can be passed on to others about the resources necessary to successfully oversee the birth of new services for widows. Obtaining funding and laying the groundwork take a long time.

The next problem was making the service known to potential clients. This was attempted chiefly through press releases, mailings to interested professionals in the area (lawyers, doctors, clergymen, and insurance agents), and contact with other local voluntary agencies. The growth of clientele was quite slow, as had been anticipated, since any new service has to become known in the community and establish recognition and confidence among potential clients. There are at least three reasons why the Widows Consultation Center may have encountered even more difficulties than other agencies, however:

1. The intermediaries to whom letters were sent apparently failed to pass on the information to widows. Only a handful of clients resulted from the hundreds of letters initially mailed to local professionals.

2. Widows are frequently told by others to "pull yourself out of it" and frequently seem to think that it is an admission of failure or inadequacy, or at the very least that it is humiliating, to come to a professional agency to ask for help with personal problems. As one widow explained her doubt that the Center could be of help: "After all, no one can help you with your problems. If you have problems, you have to work them out for yourself. That is, if you're an adult."

3. The American resistance to asking for help is compounded in the case of a new and unknown organization by the suspicion and insecurity widows are likely to feel as a part of the bereavement crisis. There is often a fear of being vulnerable, of strangers taking advantage of them in order to make money.

The problem of having only a small number of clients limited the ability of the Center to serve widows during the first year. This was eventually solved by extensive press publicity and television and radio advertising, and by the end of the second year, the Center began to be booked full for at least a week in advance.

INDIVIDUAL COUNSELLING

The Center's operations began with individual casework, with first one caseworker, then two; then an additional worker for three days a week. The first few months of effort included the collection of a library of resource materials and the establishment of contacts with other private and government agencies in the city to whom referrals might be made for specific kinds of problems.

The particular concern of the Widows Consultation Center is to provide a central source of help to eliminate, as far as possible, the frustration and despair experienced in going from one agency to another in a search for information, direction, and assistance.

Individual counselling with a caseworker may include referrals or assistance in dealing with agencies such as the Social Security Administration or the New York Housing Authority, or it may involve counselling on emotional, social, or family problems. For the former, counselling rarely goes beyond one session. For the latter cases, counselling generally involves many interviews.

An individual consultation is arranged by appointment with a social worker, although the Director is available to handle "walk-ins." In the course of this initial interview (or at later interviews), the widow's problems, which are usually multiple, are sorted out, and the widow is helped to recognize the real from the imaginary or exaggerated, the insurmountable from those that can be solved, and to determine which problems take priority. She may then be helped to take the necessary action in solving the problem(s) step by step.

These consultations are both diagnostic and therapeutic. Knowing what the real problem is and what can be done about it is viewed itself as a relief-giving experience—albeit a partial one.

Collateral casework services are one aspect of the Widows Consultation Center that distinguish it from other counselling services. This agency makes itself responsible for intervening in behalf of a widow who has met with unfair, unethical, or inadequate treatment despite every reasonable effort on her part. This might include delinquent or unpaid benefits due her, overcharges or harassment by business firms, professionals, or individuals who take advantage of supposedly unknowledgeable or defenseless widows.

When such alleged abuses are inquired into and it becomes clear that a responsible agency is concerned with a client, an adjustment is usually expedited. This activity on behalf of a widow may be a matter of a single letter or telephone call, or it may take months of negotiations and innumerable hours of compiling information, interpreting it, and communicating with government or private organizations.

OTHER SERVICES

Next to be added to the Center's services were group sessions under the leadership of professionals trained in group therapy. These meet weekly and may vary in nature, depending upon the participants and the way the group evolves, from fairly casual sharing of experiences as widows to explicitly therapeutic groups.

Social get-togethers were initiated slowly, with the first year's activities most typically a monthly tea at the Center preceded by a brief lecture on some topic of apparent interest to widows, such as a book on widowhood.

By the third year, a part-time social worker was hired to spend all of her time organizing and conducting social activities, such as a weekly Sunday afternoon session at the local "Y," weekend bus trips, and theater parties using free tickets she is able to wheedle from ticket managers.

From the beginning the Center's staff wanted to establish financial and legal guidance services through the use of professional consultants in these areas, and professional consultants were soon located and retained.

The financial consultant is a well-known writer on personal finance, who does not recommend specific investments or companies but gives general advice on types of investments, budgeting, and allocation of funds.

Legal counselling initially consisted entirely of referring clients with obvious legal problems to the Legal Referral Service of the City Bar Association. However, the Center eventually obtained a ruling from the Ethics Committee of the Bar allowing it to have a legal consultant on the staff. This consultant reviews potential legal problems with the clients and indicates those which require further attention from an attorney. He helps the widow to evaluate and understand her legal problem.

During the third year of operation, a few widows who had been helped by the Center began to do volunteer work with other widows, such as calling them on the telephone or inviting small groups to their homes for socializing.

As summarized in a statement to the Center's Board of Directors in April 1972: "The goal of all these services capsulized above is to give the widow an initial start on movement away from bereavement, confusion, immobility, isolation, lack of motivation; and to then help her move away from the protective environment of this agency and reach out to others in her community in an effort to rebuild her life."

After two and a half years, the Center saw many potential areas of expansion, such as a newsletter, more expansion of volunteer services, and initiation of special job-training programs through securing special group rates for widows at secretarial or other schools. However, these new programs awaited further funding. At the end of the three-year pilot period, the Prudential declined to continue to be the sole source of financing. Though believing that the Widows Consultation Center had demonstrated a real need for the services it provided, the Prudential felt that it had done its part—and more—by paying for the three pilot years.

The Prudential officers felt that the pilot project had demonstrated that it met a need and that it worked, but also that it was up to others to participate in the support of the New York Center or to fund similar projects elsewhere.

3

THE EVALUATION RESEARCH METHODS

Because this was a pilot social service project, it was not reasonable or ethical to set up rigid experimental and control groups in order to evaluate its effectiveness. The purpose of the evaluation research was to obtain a record of exactly what the Center was doing and a rough idea of the effectiveness of these services as they developed. Extensive anonymous case history data and interviews with staff members were relied upon as the main source of data about the Center's operations, supplemented by official records and minutes as well as tape recordings of group therapy sessions.

The effectiveness of the services was evaluated on the basis of a follow-up interview, attempted with all clients who visited the Center from the time it opened until the end of November 1971. The interviews took place from three months to one and a half years after the initial visit to the Center. The widows' own reports during these follow-up interviews about whether they were helped in solving various types of problems serve as the main criteria for the effectiveness of the Center's efforts.

The follow-up interviews with the widows, despite some reservations by the staff that these might cause emotional distress, generally seem to have been a good experience for the respondents, giving them a supportive audience for talking about themselves. Overall, the response rate for those who were contacted was 77%. Analysis of the reasons for refusal offered by those who did not grant an interview shows that in most cases, the refusal represents resistance to the interview process itself rather than a negative reaction to the Center as the subject of the interview.

The rest of this chapter is an overview of the evaluation research methods used, and the problems encountered, in order to give the reader an understanding of the origins and possible limitations of the data from the study after measurement of their problems to the rest (the no-help, or control group). This was felt by all involved to be ethically unacceptable, especially which are reported in subsequent chapters. For those who are interested in doing an evaluation of services to widows which would produce comparable results, more details of the research procedures, including the case history and client follow-up interview forms, appear in Appendixes B and C.

THE RESEARCH DESIGN: PRACTICAL CONSIDERATIONS AND THE RESULTANT FORM

The classic design for evaluating the effectiveness of intervention or attempts to help people is deceptively simple on the surface but totally inappropriate for a pilot project such as the Widows Consultation Center, if one looks beneath the surface at the assumptions on which such a design is based. According to the classical experimental design, one would begin with an idea of the kinds of changes in the quality of widows' lives one wished to make (the dependent variables) and a set of specific intervention or helping techniques which the staff of the agency would use on all widows in the project (the independent variables). One would begin with two groups of widows who were "matched" in the sense that, on the whole, they were similar in terms of the nature of their problems and their characteristics (age, length of widowhood, socio-economic status, etc.). One group would receive help (the experimental group), one would not (the control group). Figure 3.1 shows a classic experimental design, measuring the effectiveness of the attempt to help by seeing if there is any difference in outcome for the two groups. There are many reasons why this design and more complex control group designs are inappropriate for evaluating a pilot project like the Widows Consultation Center. As Weiss and Rein have stated:

This very plausible approach is misleading when the action programs have broad aims and unstandardized forms. We believe it may well be effective when a number of individuals are subjected to the same interventive stimulus and when the expected outcome is clear-cut and truly something anticipated. An example would be inoculation with a flu vaccine: the same thing can be done to a large number of subjects, and the expected outcome —freedom from influenza—can be stated in advance. But there are many social action programs, including most truly ambitious social action programs, which do not have these characteristics (Weiss and Rein, p. 287).

The main problems which preclude a rigorous experimental design are summarized below.

1. Lack of standardized problems and treatment. Although one can make generalizations about the kinds of problems that widows are most likely to have, there are so many, and they vary so greatly in their relative intensity and the particular combination in which they are experienced by various widows, that it becomes absurd to think that one could give them all a similar, standardized treatment.

2. *The changing nature of the services themselves.* The very nature of a pilot project involves changes over time in the nature of the services offered and the clients served. Specifically, in the case of the Widows Consultation Center, the kinds of help that widows would need, the specific programs or techniques which would be developed to provide this help, and procedures for attracting and screening clients, were conceptualized in only the broadest terms at the initiation of the project. As time passed, new services were added and changes were made in the way services were offered, on the basis of experience.

Figure 3.1
CLASSIC EXPERIMENTAL DESIGN

	Time 1	Time 2	Time 3
Experimental widows	Measure problems	Help	Measure problems
Control widows	Measure problems	No Help	Measure problems

Observe difference if any

3. *Impossibility of a control group.* Creating matched experimental and control groups of widows would have been difficult and ethically unacceptable. The widows who come to the Center for help have taken positive steps in recognizing that they have problems they are unable to resolve, and they are seeking aid. Widows who lived in the New York City area but did not contact the Center could *not* be presumed to be the same except that they did not come. Given the extensive television, radio, and newspaper coverage of the Center's existence, those who did not come must be assumed to have lesser problems or more resources for solving them or to be unwilling or unready to go to an agency and ask for assistance. In other words, one could not obtain a matched control group for interviewing by finding a sample of widows who did not come to the Center.

Conceptually, one could have taken widows who *did* come to the Center for help, and on a random basis, given help to some and only a before-and-since at no time during the first eighteen months was the demand for services so great that the Center would have had to turn away some requests for help anyhow. Such rigor would also be quite premature; the main function of a control group would be to see if changes that occur in the well-being of widows who are assisted by the Center would have occurred anyhow, rather than being due to the Center's efforts. Before looking for such alternative explanations, we need to establish whether or not the clients do seem to show any improvements or changes at all.

The evaluation research design which was worked out for the Widows Consultation Center parallels the conclusions that Weiss and Rein reached about appropriate research techniques to take the place of a rigid experimental design:

First, a more effective methodology would be much more descriptive and inductive. It would be concerned with describing the unfolding form of the experimental intervention, the reactions of individuals and institutions subjected to its impact, and the consequences, so far as they can be learned by interview and observation, for these individuals and institutions. It would lean toward the use of field methodology, emphasizing interview and observation . . . (Weiss and Rein, 1971, p. 295).

DATA COLLECTION PROCEDURES

The heart of the evaluation of the Center's efforts was a follow-up interview with the clients themselves, conducted during the period from November 1971 to June 1972. This interview focused on the widow's own perceptions of what her problems were, what the Center did, whether or not this was helpful in solving her problems, and her overall reaction to the Center. Contacts with the clients of the Center for purposes of requesting the follow-up interview were made a minimum of three months after the initial visit to the Center in order to give sufficient time for the widow to be able to give a retrospective evaluation of the impact the Center had on her. A little over half of the widows had first come to the Center from four months to a year before the follow-up interview; for the others, it had been between one and two years since the first visit.

The other main procedures and research instruments used were:

1. A case history compiled by the caseworker. At the time of a widow's first visit to the Center, each social worker attempted to cover an outlined set of topics (including potential problem areas and selected characteristics of the clients), in the course of a client-centered, nonstandardized interview. A standardized interview at the time of intake or the use of any fixed-wording questions was rejected by the staff of the Center because they believed such procedures would have alienated a large proportion of the clients. Many women came in a quite distraught state, and needed to pour out their problems in a conversational manner, rather than answering a highly structured questionnaire. Following the initial consultation, the caseworker filled in a standardized case history form. This was then updated to include subsequent visits and contacts, detailing additional problems or information about the widow which the caseworker learned, and the nature of the efforts of the Center staff to help her. Copies of the case histories, with identifying information removed, were coded for the purpose of the evaluation, and the originals remained at the Center for reference during subsequent visits of the client to the Center.

2. *Interviews with members of the staff.* The founders, director, caseworkers, and other staff members of the Center were interviewed in a nondirective manner at various times during the pilot project to find out about problems, successes, and new developments. At the end of the evaluation period, the two group therapy leaders and all caseworkers were interviewed, using an interview guide in order to systematically cover all areas for which information was desired.

3. *Taping of group discussion sessions.* All sessions of the widows' discussion groups were recorded with the knowledge of the participants. The tapes were then used both to obtain more insight into the feelings of the clients of the Center and as a basis for describing the nature of the discussion group as a helping technique. The voluminous collection of cassette tapes which resulted would not have been necessary for the evaluation; several blocks of, say, ten sessions for four different groups would have been sufficient. However, once the recordings were begun, other uses were found for them. They provided a way for the director to monitor the performance of the group discussion leaders. The leaders were able to take them home in order to be able to review what had occurred before the next week's session. The recordings also served as a means of facilitating the transfer of a group to a new leader when this became necessary. These unforeseen "feedbacks" of data collected for the evaluation thus became immediately useful for the project and should be encouraged in similar evaluation efforts.

4. *Workload data and other documents.* Extensive records were kept by the staff on the activities of the Center and reported to the evaluators on a monthly basis. These included data on the number of inquiries received, number of appointments for initial consultations, number of return visits, attendance at group discussion sessions, number of consultations with financial or legal resource persons connected with the Center, etc. Other types of documents made available included copies of the minutes of the meetings of the board of directors and copies of publicity materials.

5. Direct Observation. Occasional visits were also made to the Center to observe "what was going on" and to talk with members of the staff on an informal basis. Problems of limited time and of distance from the Center made such participant observation a much more infrequent occurrence than would have been desirable.

THE NATURE OF THE EVALUATIVE CRITERIA

Most of the measurements of "success" or "improvement" in this study are based upon the subjective perceptions of the widow herself and secondarily upon perceptions of staff members as to the degree of helpfulness of the Center's various efforts. Whenever possible, more objective criteria were also collected, however. If the widow needed a job when she came to the Center and had one at the time of the follow-up interview that she had obtained through the Center, one has an objective basis for saying her job situation has improved. Another example of an area where objective measures could be used would be in intervention with Social Security or other agencies. If the case record showed that a woman came with a problem such as a refusal by Social Security to pay benefits; that the Center made telephone calls and wrote letters on the widow's behalf; and that subsequently the widow began receiving benefits, one could say that there is objective evidence that this problem was improved. In most problem areas, however, the basis for evaluation of the Center's efforts can only be the widow's own subjective opinion as to whether the Center helped her deal with her problem. It may be argued that this is not always a valid criterion: that, for instance, a particular widow is really better balanced emotionally after having talked about her feelings at the Center, and that she is mistaken when she says the Center was not helpful to her. However, the client is in the best situation to report whether or not she was helped or how the services offered were inadequate for solving her problems. A fairly well established principle in social casework is that "in the final analysis, client appraisals will, or at least should be, an important determinant of the kinds of services offered" (Mayer and Timms, 1970, p. 3).

In the past, most attempts at evaluation of the effectiveness of social services have been based upon the judgments of social workers rather than clients. The director and workers at the Center also felt that they would know whether or not they have helped their clients, and that there was no reason to have to ask the clients themselves for their opinions on the assumption that

the judgments of the practitioner and those of the clients would coincide. This might seem a reasonable assumption, but, on inspection, it turns out to be in large measure wrong. A review of the few studies in which relevant comparisons can be made reveals marked disparities between the two sets of judgments (Mayer and Timms, 1970, p. 3).

As a matter of fact, there turned out to be almost total agreement between the reports of caseworkers and those of clients about the areas in which the Center had been most effective. This agreement gives us added confidence in the data.

CLIENT PROTECTION: PROCEDURES USED IN CONDUCTING THE FOLLOW-UP INTERVIEWS

The professional staff of the Center was initially concerned about having its clients contacted for follow-up interviews, on the grounds that the release of their names to interviewers would be a breach of confidentiality and that being interviewed could be emotionally distressing.

To satisfy the first of these objections, elaborate steps were taken to protect the clients' right to privacy. Before any names of clients were released, each widow received a letter explaining the nature of the study and enclosing a postcard form on which she could check, "I do not wish to be interviewed." In that case, her name was not released by the Center at all. Besides those clients who returned the postcard refusal form, the caseworkers at the Center reviewed the case histories of all of their own clients and designated those that they thought were too emotionally distraught or disturbed to be interviewed without becoming upset. Sixty-three clients were not contacted at all on the basis of this consideration.

Careful steps were taken to protect the confidentiality of information given by those widows who did agree to be interviewed. The name and address of the clients appeared only on a separate top sheet to the interview. Before the interview was coded or could be seen by anyone not directly involved in the follow-up interviews, this identifying information was removed from the top sheet by the personnel at the Center and replaced with the case history number.

The staff of the Center were also concerned that even though they had tried to screen out the most emotionally fragile clients, the interview might reactivate feelings of grief and distress for many clients, especially if the interview were not handled with great sensitivity. These concerns were formally expressed in a letter to the evaluators by the sponsors, who had become chairman and president of the Center:

In the interests of arriving at a sound evaluation, of good public relations, and above all, our profound concern with the feelings of already traumatized individuals, we would emphasize the importance of selecting skilled interviewers, sensitive to the fact that these are women who have, in most cases, not yet recovered from a devastating experience.

Few women with bereavement problems are free from loneliness, grief or anxiety for the first few years.

Aside from our responsibility to the individual clients, we as a new agency which has to concern itself with its image as a compassionate consultation and treatment center, are deeply aware of the importance of subjecting clients to the most sensitive and knowledgeable interviewers available.

Only experienced, mature interviewers were recruited for the project. After pretesting by the evaluator, three women were selected to conduct the personal interviews. One had a master's degree in social work and the other two had extensive training and interviewing experience with National Opinion Research Center and other survey research organizations.

The concerns of the Center's staff might have been alleviated if Lopata's study of widows had been available at the time. She describes how she had similar reservations about interviewing emotionally fragile widows and how this was resolved (Lopata, 1973, p. x).

Dr. Erich Lindemann who pioneered work in this field . . . convinced me that widows need to talk about their feelings and problems and that the interviews which I had planned with them would be beneficial rather than harmful.

Dr. Lindemann believes strongly that modern urban societies deprive the griever of many opportunities to do grief work, a process which requires talking about personal reactions to death, about the deceased, about the whole series of events leading to death, and about the life changes that follow it. Thus, the interview could have a therapeutic effect on the widow, as well as provide information which could benefit other women in the same situation.

The interviewers were carefully monitored to make sure that the experience was not turning out to be a distressing one for the widows, by having the interviewers return all completed interviews immediately and complete a report form on the interviewing experience.

Based on the information reported on the interviewer report forms filled in for each interview and on the scarcity of complaints to the Center or the evaluator, one can say that the reaction of the clients to the interviews was generally favorable.

Of the widows interviewed, 92% were reported by the interviewers to be cooperative, and in only 3% of the interviews did the interviewer feel that the respondent was evasive or possibly untruthful. Of those interviewed, 81% did not get emotionally upset or cry at any point; 11% did get upset or cry at one point, most often at the questions on emotional adjustment; and 8% got upset and cried more than once. However, most widows were reported to find the interview an enjoyable experience on the whole because it provided them with a sympathetic ear. Most seemed to view it as an extension of the service of the Widows Consultation Center itself, a chance to talk freely and in confidence about their problems.

Examples of this "typical" reported reaction were:

"She was very cooperative and wanted to talk. It seemed to relieve her tensions."

"She enjoyed talking immensely. Told me of her childhood and gave me advice."

"I think she was candid and appreciated the opportunity to rehash her problems, especially as in many situations (she told me) she cannot talk easily."

"She viewed me as company and a help . . . She told me it was 'a relief' to talk with someone. She has no one."

The interviewers were instructed to go out of their way to make the interview experience a supportive, pleasant one for the widow, even though this might mean listening to a person "ramble on" about a problem that was bothering her, far beyond the direct response to a question which would be codable for purposes of the study. On the other hand, the interviewers were not supposed to give advice, even if asked, but to suggest that the widow might call the Center and talk to her caseworker about any problems that she asked the interviewer to help with.

Many of the interviewed widows were quite lonely, physically sick, or emotionally distressed, and they grasped at the human contact the interviewer offered. This made the breaking off of the interview difficult in many cases. The interviewers were instructed to spend extra time at the end of the interview to make the respondent "feel good," if necessary. For example, one interviewer reported, "Mrs. F. was very upset during the interview. By the last question she was in tears. I put aside the interview and asked her to make coffee for us, which she did, and when I left, she had regained her composure."

Occasionally, the interviewer stumbled into a crisis situation which could not be ignored. In a few cases, the widow began talking about suicide, for instance. This raised a problem of protecting the confidentiality of the information given the interviewer, versus the possible carrying out of the threat if no one responded to it. A compromise situation was reached, whereby the caseworker of the widow who threatened suicide was contacted, told that the widow seemed "very depressed" or suicidal but not told any of the details, and asked to call the widow and inquire generally about her well-being.

Another example of the occasional crisis situation into which the interviewer stumbled and felt compelled to deal with was as follows:

Mrs. D. was periodically confused and preoccupied during the interview . . . Finally, in response to her last two answers I asked again what was the matter. . . She then opened up. She apparently had been feeling dreadful the last two days. She wanted to go to the hospital. . . I encouraged Mrs. D. to call her daughter . . . helped her to plan the call, find the number, plan how to get to the hospital . . . I then spent half an hour helping her to get ready to go to the hospital—dress warmly, find the $20 she had misplaced, etc.

Those women who did react negatively to the interview tended to do so because they misunderstood the purpose, even though it was carefully explained in advance, and thought that the interviewer was a member of the staff of the Center who was coming to visit in order to help them. An example of this occasional reaction was: "If I knew it was going to be like this I would never have let you come. I'm not going to get anything out of it. I thought you came from the Center to talk things over with me."

More typically, the widows tended to agree to participate in the study because "The Center helped me, and I'd be glad to do something for them," and found the interview itself turned out to be an enjoyable experience on the whole.

Overall the response rate for those who were contacted for the follow-up interviews was 77%. A complete breakdown of the research outcome for the entire group is shown in Table 3.1.

Table 3.1

Results of Interview Attempts

Personal interviews	140	32%
Completed telephone interviews	84	19%
Incomplete telephone interviews	35	8%
Refused interview	79	18%
WCC excluded	63	14%
Could not locate	38	9%
TOTAL	439	100%

Source: Widows Consultation Center records and face sheet of interview records (see Appendix C, item 3).

The almost 10% of clients who could not be located, despite the fact that their address and telephone number were asked for at the time of first visit to the Center, seems quite high at first glance. Efforts were made through such sources as the telephone company, post office, and apartment house superintendents to find new address information for widows who appeared to have moved, but there were still thirty-eight women who were not reached at all during the interviewing period. This is to be expected, however, given the greater than average tendency of the newly widowed to relocate. Many of them had moved out of the metropolitan area or had left no forwarding address. In many other cases, the widow had an unlisted telephone number which she never reported to the Center, or else changed to an unlisted phone number after her visit to the Center. (This problem of unlisted telephones is probably much more prevalent in the New York City area than it would be elsewhere.) Also included in this category of unable to locate or contact are widows for whom an apparently current telephone number or address was obtained, but who were not home or repeatedly did not answer the telephone.

FACTORS ASSOCIATED WITH REFUSALS TO BE INTERVIEWED

What characteristics of clients are associated with their having completed a follow-up interview or not?

For all those widows who could be located, we have a potential source of information about reasons for refusal. Widows who returned the postcard to the Center checking "I do not wish to be interviewed" had a place for "comments." For those who did not refuse by postcard but refused when contacted by telephone for an appointment, the interviewer was to record the reason for refusal.

Twenty-one widows who returned the postcards did make comments. Only four of these were negative, saying that the Center had not helped them. Ten gave reasons such as having a new job with irregular hours or having moved to Florida. Eight gave praise of the Center, but no explanation of why they did not wish to be contacted. Typical of these comments accompanying refusals were:

"The service is enlightening and helpful in many ways." "They helped me when I needed it."

The reasons for refusal recorded by interviewers follow the same pattern. Most refer to reasons why the interview itself was not convenient or acceptable to them, rather than expressing reactions to the Center as the proposed subject of the interview. Such reasons included being too busy, ill health, or having moved. (Examples: "I'm in no mood for conversation." "I have no time. I'm working and fine now. I don't need the Center anymore." "I'm not interested in anybody interviewing me now. I had no friends then but now I have more than enough.")

Eight made positive comments about the Center while refusing, such as "My experience was very satisfying. Mrs. X. was wonderful. But I don't have time now." Another comment along this line was, "Just talking to you people at the time was very helpful. But it's in the past." Nine made negative comments about the Center and gave this as the reason for not wanting to be interviewed, including five who said they got nothing from the Center, so why should they give their time? Typical of these refusals based on negative feelings about the Center was the heated reaction: "I'll have nothing to do with them. They were horrible. They wanted to know all about me. You ask them for help and they ask you all kinds of personal questions."

Based on these comments accompanying refusals, one can conclude that those clients who refused to be interviewed were probably somewhat more likely to have negative feelings about the Center than were those who cooperated, but the majority were positively disposed toward the Center and refused for other reasons. Only thirteen (16%) of the seventy-nine who refused expressed negative attitudes toward the Center.

The outcome of the attempt to interview clients was significantly related to many characteristics of the clients, including age, years widowed, race, deceased husband's occupation, which caseworker a woman had, and the nature of the husband's death. Women over sixty-five were more than twice as likely as widows under forty-five to refuse to be interviewed (23% versus 10% refusals). Widows under fifty-five were much more likely than the average client to have a telephone interview rather than a personal interview, because their working hours made it more difficult to arrange a personal visit. The more recently widowed, the more likely a client was to complete an interview, especially a personal interview.

Blacks were more likely to have telephone interviews than personal interviews, and no blacks were excluded from contacts on the basis of "emotional fragility." (This was a very interesting finding, but the reasons for it can only be guessed at.) Those whose deceased husbands were in blue-collar occupations were most likely to complete personal interviews, while white-collar widows were more likely to refuse to be interviewed at all. In relation to the cause of the husband's death, those whose husbands died in accidents were least likely to complete a personal interview and most likely to agree to answer only a few questions on the telephone, compared to those whose husbands had died of natural causes. One can speculate that those who had lost their husbands in accidents were the least able to accept the deaths and most likely to be reluctant to reopen feelings of grief.

Though these differences all mean that the interviewed clients are somewhat different from those who were not, one cannot say that there is a clear direction in which they will distort the results of the follow-up interviews.

In addition, there is a strong relationship between the number of times a client came to the Center and the likelihood of completing the follow-up interview. Only 27% of those who came to the Center just once completed a personal interview, compared to 87% of those who came back five or more times for consultations, group therapy, etc. This means that clients who found the Center helpful and who were given the most time and assistance are somewhat overrepresented in the results of the interviews, and this should be kept in mind in assessing the results.

On the other hand, a contrasting limitation of the interview data is that since the Center was constantly developing its program, the "follow-up" widows did not receive the benefit of the developments which took place during the second half of the three-year pilot project. In particular, many fewer of the initial clients were encouraged to return to the Center for additional consultation after the first visit, and the social activities program had just begun to get off the ground. Only 12% of the clients in the follow-up survey had visited the Center more than once. As will be discussed in a later section on the casework process, the policy toward return visits changed after the first year. By the third year, one can estimate that at least half of the clients were receiving more than one consultation. Thus, the fact that widows who visited the Center more than once were more likely to complete a personal interview is more than offset by the fact that the total client group served by the Center over the first five years includes a much larger proportion of these multiple visit cases than did the initial client group interviewed.

OTHER LIMITATIONS

It should be reiterated that the evaluation of the Center was done only for the first three years of operation, the pilot period financed by Prudential. Within this period the client follow-up interviews covered only the first year and a half's clients. None of the data here can be assumed to accurately describe the Center's current programs and clients, since many changes have taken place in the last two years; changes which have not been studied or documented here.

The second major limitation is that the officers and director of the Center were opposed to the extensive nature of the research required as a condition of funding. (One can hardly blame them. Who wants to be constantly questioned and watched?) The requests for generalizations about the way in which the Center treats clients were met with the reaction that it is impossible to generalize. "There is no one way to help people," insists the director. "I cannot give it to you in a nutshell." She feels that the attempt to boil things down into a kind of cookbook may actually be harmful if inexperienced social workers try to follow the recipe blindly.

The Center is thus strongly opposed to the publication of the results of the evaluation, particularly of such normally private information as candid comments in unguarded moments and of detailed budgetary information, including staff salary data. In addition, they have expressed the opinion through much of the evaluation research project that a sociologist could not possibly evaluate clinical casework procedures and group discussions. (Of course, the logical extension of this argument that "it takes one to study one" would mean that anthropologists and sociologists could not study any group except themselves.)

The adversary relationship which developed between the staff and the evaluator has undoubtedly influenced the quantity and quality of data, compared to what might have been obtained under ideal (but probably impossible) conditions of total cooperation and agreement on priorities between researcher and practitioner. For further discussion of the stresses and strains which marked the evaluation process, see Appendix B.

4

PROBLEMS IN ATTRACTING CLIENTS AND SETTING POLICIES

A major problem for the Widows Consultation Center during its initial period of operation was attracting clients. There were thousands of recent widows in the metropolitan area, but how could they be made aware of the existence of a new service which might be able to help them, and motivated to call or come?

The first strategy was to reach widows through those intermediaries who would be most likely to be in contact with them during the period in which they needed help—doctors, lawyers, clergymen, psychiatrists, monument makers, and social agencies. Over twelve hundred letters were sent to individuals in these categories, selected from professional and general directories, with a brochure on the Widows Consultation Center enclosed (see Figure 4.1). The effort bore very little fruit; only a few clients and inquiries were obtained by these letters. One can guess that what happened in many cases was that the professional read the letter, didn't know of any widows needing help at that moment, and threw it away. There is also probably a great deal of suspicion about "sales pitches" arriving through a mass produced letter—even if the service being described is a nonprofit one.

The Center then turned to the mass media. Initially there was a press conference on October 28, 1970, which was attended by UPI representatives and other journalists. Articles appeared in many newspapers, magazines, and professional journals throughout the country, as well as foreign language papers and magazines, including *The New York Times*, *The New York Post*, *The Newark News*, and *McCalls*. A tally by Prudential's public relations department in February 1971 showed that these stories had appeared in 103 publications, reaching an audience of over 16 million people in thirty-one states.

Figure 4.1

ORIGINAL BROCHURE OF WIDOWS CONSULTATION CENTER

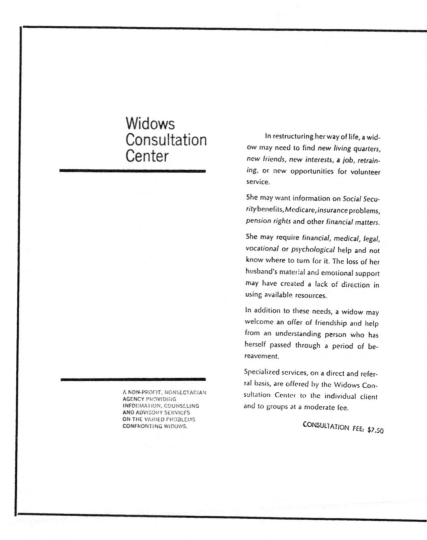

Widows
Consultation
Center

In restructuring her way of life, a widow may need to find *new living quarters, new friends, new interests, a job, retraining,* or new opportunities for volunteer service.

She may want information on *Social Security* benefits, *Medicare, insurance* problems, *pension rights* and other *financial matters.*

She may require *financial, medical, legal, vocational* or *psychological* help and not know where to turn for it. The loss of her husband's material and emotional support may have created a lack of direction in using available resources.

In addition to these needs, a widow may welcome an offer of friendship and help from an understanding person who has herself passed through a period of bereavement.

Specialized services, on a direct and referral basis, are offered by the Widows Consultation Center to the individual client and to groups at a moderate fee.

CONSULTATION FEE: $7.50

A NON-PROFIT, NONSECTARIAN
AGENCY PROVIDING
INFORMATION, COUNSELING
AND ADVISORY SERVICES
ON THE VARIED PROBLEMS
CONFRONTING WIDOWS.

Figure 4.2
REVISED BROCHURE OF WIDOWS CONSULTATION CENTER

"It doesn't seem real or possible that my husband's dead."

The unreality of death, the need to accept the unacceptable can be fully understood only by those faced with similar disaster. Even being able to air such feelings openly, knowing they will be understood and shared, can relieve enormous inner pressures.

"I've been trying hard but not making much progress alone".

Widows don't get enough credit for their efforts. Too often people say of her, "She's just not trying to adjust." The problem may be that she is trying alone, when she doesn't have to. There are others who can help her — women who are going through precisely the same things.and professional consultants who can serve as guides.

"Why is it taking me so long?"

Grief and adjustment to widowhood do not work on strict timetables. While one woman will begin to pick up the threads of her life and work out new patterns in a matter of months, many others will find a year or two have passed with little movement. Or, as has happened often, a woman will make a seemingly excellent adjustment for a year or even several years and then, suddenly, she is assailed again with the grief and fears of widowhood. It helps to talk with those who understand that recovery from grief varies with each individual.

widows
consultation . . .
center

136 EAST 57th STREET
NEW YORK, NEW YORK 10022

TELEPHONE (212) 688-8850

* * *

WIDOWS CONSULTATION CENTER . . .

*. . . to help you find
a new way of life
. . . to assure you that
you are not alone.*

ABOUT THE CENTER

The Widows Consultation Center is a non-profit, non-sectarian agency providing widows, on an individual or group basis, with information, counseling and advisory services on varied problems confronting them.

* * * * *

HOW YOU CAN GET HELP

Appointments may be arranged by telephone

Call 688-8850 Monday thru Friday
9:30am — 5:00pm

Fee per session — $15.00

Special financial arrangements are based upon ability to pay.

* * * * *

136 E. 57th St., New York, N.Y. 10022

PROBLEMS

• *Loneliness*
A besetting fear of widowhood is being alone. At the same time the new widow is often uncomfortable in the company of couples. Loneliness breeds other problems — self-pity, self-doubt, estrangement from people — and more loneliness.

• *Family Relationships*
In addition to coping with grief and loneliness, the widow may have to adjust to a new and difficult role — that of the single parent. She has to accept the weight of added responsibility while overwhelmed with feelings of dependency, of fear of being a burden to her children. She may feel neglected or may look to her children or other relatives for emotional support they cannot give.

• *Filling the void*
Before widowhood, most women centered their activities around their husbands and homes. Their lives had focus and direction. With the loss of her husband, a woman's life is shattered. Her need, now, is to rebuild her world, redirect her interest and energies.

• *Financial concerns*
These can take several forms: reduced income, lack of experience in financial affairs, and unrealistic feelings of poverty.
Some women may need help in making new arrangements to adjust to the reality of decreased income. Some need help in financial matters which their husbands always attended to. Some need assurance that their financial fears have no basis in fact.

• *Legal Difficulties*
The varied legal problems that often arise may create confusion and anxiety.

THE CENTER HELPS BY PROVIDING . . .

• *Communication with Other people*
The Center helps through group sessions to discuss mutual problems. Small groups under professional leadership meet to share feelings and experiences. Rea friendships often grow out of such group participation.

• *Shared knowledge*
It helps enormously to know how others are coping with similar problems. Small groups, under a trained leader, offer members an opportunity to express their feelings, gain knowledge of themselves, and develop better relations with others.
Other family members, through individual counseling or family sessions, can air problems that otherwise might go unresolved.

• *Vocational advice*
The woman who has not worked for years can get advice on where to go for re-training and placement. The Center also has close contact with many agencies that need volunteers.

• *Financial consultation*
Practical advice, through the services of a financial consultant, is available to the widow who needs sound guidance on the best use of her resources.
Although the Center does not provide financial assistance, help is available in coping with such practical problems as social security, insurance and pension benefits, or working out a budget.

• *Legal Advice*
An experienced lawyer is on staff to advise the widow about her legal rights and options and how to obtain legal representation if required.

A problem with this type of publicity was that it mostly reached people who were not in the New York City area. Another problem was that such articles would usually produce a brief flurry of inquiries, but they were "one-shot deals." If a woman didn't happen to feel in need of help at the time she read the article, she probably forgot all about it. There were some exceptions, of course. For instance, during the follow-up interviews, one widow who had seen a newspaper article said that she tore it out and put it in a drawer. Several months later when there was a family crisis, she remembered about the clipping, called, and made an appointment.

What was needed was some way of producing a *steady* flow of information to the community which would be likely to reach prospective clients whenever they felt in need of help. With considerable effort and personal contacts by the officers of the Center, arrangements were made for regular public service spot announcements to appear on radio and television stations in the metropolitan area: WOR, WOR-TV, WNEW, WCBS, WCBS-TV, WHN, WINS, WABC, WABC-TV, WPIX, WNBC, and WNBC-TV. The radio spots were by Center personnel, and the television spots featured Helen Hayes and Harriet van Horne. Typical of these broadcast announcements was the following, which was broadcast by WCBS-AM in the fall of 1970:

Are you a widow or do you know a widow who may need help during the period of her bereavement and thereafter? The Widows Consultation Center, a new, nonprofit, nonsectarian agency, is prepared to help widows cope with such problems as loneliness, finances, job seeking or retraining, family difficulties, and the like. A professional staff, including consultants in various fields, is available for individual and group consultation. The Widows Consultation Center is located at 136 East 57th Street, corner Lexington Avenue, New York 10022, telephone number 688-8850. You are welcome to call for an appointment or for a brochure describing the services of the Widows Consultation Center. Call 688-8850.

The stations did not keep complete records, but they used the announcements several times every day, every day of the week, at different hours of the day and night. Spot announcements of twenty, thirty, and sixty seconds duration were prepared in order to facilitate such frequent use. Fairly complete records were kept by WNEW, and they showed, for example, that during one week in May 1972 they played the announcement seventeen times, of which twelve were between midnight and 6 A.M., most likely a time during which there is a dearth of paid advertising. Overall, during the month of May 1972, WNEW played these announcements forty-nine times, and the cost would have been over $800 for that month if billed at commercial rates. Another record kept by WOR-TV showed that thirty- or sixty-second spots were played fifty times between January and March of 1972 and would have cost $19,800 if billed at commercial rates. The radio and television stations play such public service announcements and keep such records in order to help document their role in providing public service when it is time for the Federal Communications Commission to renew their broadcasting licenses. Any new agency or service should invest in producing such high-quality spot announcements to take advantage of this free advertising source. The spots are very effective, especially if a celebrity such as Helen Hayes is willing to donate the taping. She caught people's attention, helped them remember the name "Widows Consultation Center," and is respected and revered by the audience of women to whom the message is addressed. (In fact, many people to whom I have spoken about the Center have asked, "Oh, yes. Isn't that the Helen Hayes organization?")

It does not really matter that such spot announcements will appear mostly late at night or in the early morning hours; remember that one practically universal symptom of bereavement is difficulty in sleeping. The following kinds of accounts were given by clients when asked how they first heard of the agency:

"I couldn't sleep. I was terribly depressed and used to listen to the radio all the time—so I was listening and it was on the air . . ."

"Every woman who has lost her husband feels loneliness. I heard it on the radio at 3 A.M. At that moment I was at a low ebb. In the morning I called."

"I heard it on CBS radio. At that time the word 'widow' still made me shudder. I really didn't accept it. Normally I wouldn't go to an agency or anything like that, but I heard the ad several times and it seemed like it was aimed at *me*."

This constant radio and television coverage generated large numbers of calls for information or advice, and also the majority of clients who came for at least one personal consultation, as shown in Tables 4.1 and 4.2. (Since the television spots were not begun until the fall of 1971, the full impact is not visible in the figures for clients through the end of 1971.)

At about the same time, the brochure was redesigned by a public relations professional. This new brochure was sent out to all who inquired by telephone or letter about the Center, and it gave much more information about the kinds of services offered and the cost for the client. This new brochure was based on the experiences gained during the first months of operation and was felt by the staff to be more informative and effective. Portions of it are reproduced in Figure 4.2.

The Canadian Centre also found that "normal" publicity channels were inadequate, but its eventual decision was to abandon the whole service model whereby widows have to seek out a central source of help. The Canadian Centre had the usual numerous one-shot newspaper, radio, and television publicity plus the distribution of brochures, following its opening in

Table 4.1

Source of Information about or Referral to the Widows Consultation Center (June 1970 - December 1971)

Source	%
Radio	48
Television	9
Newspaper	11
Magazine	4
Friend or relative	15
Another client	1
Other social services	3
Minister, lawyer, doctor	2
No answer	7
TOTAL	100 (462 clients)

Source: Intake interviews.

Table 4.2
Source of Telephone Inquiries
(Two-month sample)

Source	May 1972		May 1973	
	Number	%	Number	%
Television	167	57	214	60
Radio	94	31	49	14
Individual	25	8	45	13
Newspaper, magazine	5	2	38	11
Other agency	4	2	9	2
Not recorded	555	––	637	––
TOTAL	850	100	992	100

Source: Widows Consultation Center records.

May 1974. Some months later, their director concluded,

In spite of this, initial response was slow, and it became apparent that widows are a group not easily reached by publicity alone. Beginning in November, a more continuous flow of publicity was provided through a thirty-second spot announcement on radio and television. Although this stimulated a greater response to the service, the validity of the original concept, i.e., one limited to professional counselling on client request, was questioned. Consequently... in response to perceived need in the client group... widow-to-widow service was added, which is based on aggressive outreach to recent widows located through obituary notices (DeGraves, 1975).

It is my own conclusion that most programs should have such an outreach program from the beginning, although in New York City there are so many widows that the Center was eventually able to attract as many clients as it could handle by reliance on the mass media.

INTAKE PROCEDURES

Once a fairly large flow of inquiries had been generated, the problem arose of how to handle them. By October 1971, there was no specific pattern followed. Many called with such vague inquiries as "What is this widow thing?" especially if they had seen only a thirty-second television spot. The two part-time receptionists tried to draw out the problems the widows might have and always tried to work in a mention that there was a $12.50 consultation fee which would be reduced if the potential client could not afford it. If there were specific questions, the caller was transferred to any available social worker, who might handle the problem then or refer the caller to an agency more properly suited to the problem. If the caller requested an appointment, it was made, but more generally a brochure was sent and she was asked to call back after she had read it if she wished an appointment with a consultant.

SCREENING APPLICANTS

A problem arose because of the "broad net" cast by the television and radio publicity. The Center was not set up to deal directly with problems of economic need or health, but these disclaimers did not come through on the mass media. As one of the caseworkers put it in January 1971, "The people coming in as a result of the CBS spot are basically women who are poor, lonely, and long-time widows." Should the Center set up appointments with anyone who happened to be a widow?

The staff of the Center tended toward wanting to schedule appointments with as many widows as possible, as long as their time was not fully occupied. The Prudential, in its dual role as funder and evaluator, began to insist that this was not a proper use of the Center's resources. After a long period of discussion, the problem was "officially" resolved by a written policy agreement in March 1971, in a letter from Martin Albaum to the Chairman and President of the Center:

We have had several long discussions of the need of the Widows Consultation Center to accept as clients only those widows whom there is a fair chance it can help. I believe that we all agree that the WCC cannot try to deal with all the problems that widows may have both because of its limited resources and also because some problems are not likely to be alleviated by counselling. These considerations were recognized explicitly in the proposal that was submitted to Prudential when it said "Widows whose main needs are brought about by either age or poverty will be referred to the numerous services that try to deal with these problems." Of course, it is possible that the widow who has needs that are occasioned by poverty or old age might also be helped by the WCC in dealing with other concerns.

In a more positive way, I think that all the WCC's publicity ought to stress counselling aimed at helping the widow to adjust to widowhood, and any criteria for screening out clients ought to start from this premise. The WCC's brochure does start here when it begins "In restructuring her way of life, the widow. . . ." But in screening potential clients, more explicit criteria are needed. I would assume that a woman who has been a widow less than three years is still in the process of adjusting. Three years may be the wrong period, but judging from the current data, it is probably a good starting place. We can adjust the period on the basis of the WCC's further experience. For those applicants who have been widowed more than three years, appointments for personal interviews should not be granted if the problems fall *exclusively* into the following categories:
1. old age, or physical or mental infirmity
2. poverty
3. the cost or adequacy of housing, or relations with landlord
4. dealing with government agencies
An applicant who falls into these categories should be referred to agencies that can help her with her problems.

A system was begun of filtering all intake interviews through a caseworker acting as a telephone receptionist. Eventually, however, this was stopped by the Center. The explanations given by the staff fall into four categories: (1) it was cutting down on the number of clients too much, since so many had their questions answered on the telephone; (2) it was too time-consuming for the caseworker; (3) the professional caseworkers probably felt some embarrassment or status conflict in sitting at the switchboard in a "non-professional" appearing capacity; and (4) the caseworkers really felt that they could be of potential help to all widows, even if they were deemed "inappropriate" by the official intake policy.

Below are some comments made by the caseworkers in the fall of 1972 which explain why the intake procedures were switched back to the original system of generally being handled by the receptionist, who switches new clients to the director if she is available.

"We were attempting to screen out some of the telephone inquiries initially and almost doing an intake on the telephone. This was requiring a great deal of our time because we encouraged the person to talk in an effort to understand what their need was and then tried to set up an appointment if the problem seemed to require it. This was taking a great deal of our time and we were more or less expanding at that . . . [in addition], sometimes consciously or unconsciously they don't give you the full statement on the phone."

"A widow to me is a widow, regardless of her age. I think that there is much that we can do, because basic to all of these people is a need for emotional support. Regardless of the concrete problem is the need for support and for someone to just listen. Even if you can't handle their housing complaint, to be able to ventilate with somebody who is willing to listen to these frustrations, gains something for the person, another lifeline. As far as poverty or old age, you can still see the older woman and give her a reason for going on."

Screening procedures for potential clients remained spotty, and they represent a problem that was never satisfactorily resolved. The lack of rigorous screening meant that the possibility of refusing help to a widow who could really benefit was greatly reduced. However, as will be seen in the chapter on the casework process, it also meant that the caseworkers began to feel drained by a constant flow of a large number of new cases. In addition, with the telephone intake or screening frequently placed in the hands of the nonprofessional receptionists, there is the problem that their judgments of who is in need of the service and can benefit from it may differ from the judgments that would be made by a social worker.

CANCELLATIONS AND NO-SHOWS

Another problem which was never successfully resolved was that a high proportion of widows who made an appointment called and cancelled it later or just never showed up at the appointed time. The extent of this problem can be seen by looking at the data for a few specific months (Table 4.3), which tend to show about three quarters of appointments kept by old clients returning for another visit, but only a little better than half of the appointments kept for first visits. (This problem is not unique to the Center. Quantified data are lacking on cancellations and no-shows for new clients of other social service agencies offering individual counselling by appointment, but the field reports of my social work interns frequently mention this problem.)

This problem came up in a discussion in December 1971. The director speculated that "Most people are suspicious and distrustful when they come. There is a very strong resistance to go to an agency on the part of many women. I think this will decrease somewhat with time, when we are better known and it will seem more acceptable to come here for help."

Caseworker: "I talked to a woman who cancelled twice. I called and asked her what was wrong. She said, 'What I want to know is who is funding this and what's the gimmick?' They are afraid that someone is trying to take advantage of them."
Evaluator: "They are reluctant?"
Caseworker: "A lot of times when they see $12.50 on the brochure, they change their minds, even though it says the fee is adjustable."

Table 4.3

Cancellations and No-Shows

Month	New Clients			Old Clients		
	Appoint-ments made	Cancelled, changed no-show	% kept	Appoint-ments made	Cancelled, changed no-show	% kept
January 1971	39	18	54	12	2	83
May 1972	113	47	58	123	35	72
March 1973	80	37	53	190	39	79

Source: Widows Consultation Center records.

Such suspicion was also voiced by one widow in the follow-up interview. She said: "It's a business, I think. They're supported by Prudential. It's worth it to them to support these expensive offices, the staff—it should bring business to them."

A receptionist commented to me when asked about the cancellation problem: "Sometimes no reason is given. Other times, the widows call and say they do not feel well or that something has come up. Not all bother to call and cancel; some just don't show up."

Putting together the cancellation and no-show data with that on initial inquiries (Tables 4.2 and 4.3), we see that in one month which does not seem atypical, May 1972, the Center received 850 telephone inquiries, mostly from ongoing or potential clients, we can assume. Of these, 236 resulted in appointments being made, and 154 of the appointments were kept by the clients. One reason for the gap between the number of potential clients making inquiries and the number of actual clients seen by the caseworkers seems to be that many widows feel that it is difficult for them to get to the Center, even though it is located near bus and subway lines. Some of the widows contacted for follow-up interviews commented on the problem that location posed for them. A Queens woman said: " I always wanted to go back, because the experience was so satisfying. But to get into Manhattan by subway is so hard. If you drive, then there is no place to park the car." A New Jersey woman who went only once said: "The difficulty is distance. I only go to the city for something really special." An elderly Brooklyn woman commented: "It is very difficult for me to use the subways. The stairs are too long and the subways are not safe." A Bronx woman said: "I wish they had a Center in the Bronx nearby that I could go to, or if it could be arranged for meetings in each other's homes." In other words, a very large proportion of widows will not travel to an unfamiliar neighborhood for help. This is why services for widows should be community based.

Another indicator that difficulty in getting to the Center may have dissuaded many potential clients is that there were so few "walk-ins," despite the fact that the address was included in most publicity. During most months in 1972 there were only three to six widows who dropped in without an appointment, and there were never more than nine.

There is probably no place in New York City that would have been any more convenient for women to reach, however. The need to rely on mass transportation and the long time and distance involved in travelling to midtown Manhattan from many other parts of the city pose a problem which is unique to New York and not solvable.

TOTAL CLIENT FLOW

By mid-1972 the Center was generally booked to capacity for a week or two in advance, with four appointments a day scheduled for each of the caseworkers, and the director available to handle walk-ins if necessary. There was some overbooking in that two clients were often scheduled in the same half-day, and if both came, it would actually take more than the three hours allotted. There were no other adjustments made, however, because it was felt that to keep a widow waiting for a caseworker more than a few minutes would severely damage the possibility for establishing rapport. The trend of the total caseload of clients is summarized in Table 4.4. The number of interviews exceeds the number of clients because some widows were seen many times during a single three-month period.

By the end of the second year of operation, the Center no longer had a problem of attracting clients, as can be seen, but rather was feeling slightly squeezed for staff time and space to handle the clients.

THE CONSULTATION FEE

Whether or not to charge a fee for individual consultation, group discussion sessions and other servies; how much to charge; and the mechanics of

Table 4.4

Growth in Clients

	No. of old Clients	No. of new Clients	Monthly average total no. of different clients	Total individual interviews conducted	Total group discussion visits
Jan.-March, 1971	43	68	37	138	47
April-June, 1971	42	59	34	122	63
July-Sept., 1971	43	73	39	151	45
Oct.-Dec., 1971	62	105	56	247	153
Jan.-March, 1972	93	119	71	318	70
April-June, 1972	146	162	103	416	178
July-Sept., 1972	129	123	84	383	117
Oct.-Dec., 1972	131	129	87	402	158
Jan.-March, 1973	189	141	110	504	189

Note: The total number of group discussion visits is the number of client visits for group discussion sessions during the quarter. If five persons attended a session one week and eight the next, the total number of group discussion visits for the two weeks would be thirteen.

Source: Widows Consultation Center records.

collecting the fee were administrative problems which prompted consideration at several points during the first years of the Center's operations. Any fee at all may deter some widows from asking for help. On the other hand, most people, it was felt, want to pay for a professional service they have received, if they can, and the charging of fees could potentially stretch the financial resources of the Center so that it could be of more service to more widows. It was also felt that in this money-oriented society, a totally free service might not be valued as highly as one which a woman paid for, and that it might deter some clients from coming on the basis of not wanting to accept "charity." The advantages of charging some sort of fee were thought to outweigh the disadvantages, and from the beginning, a policy was established of having a set fee, which could be reduced or totally waived for those women with limited income. Initially, the fee was $5; later $7.50; and by the end of 1971, $12.50, where it remained for the duration of the pilot period.

A sliding scale based on family income was developed. If the woman was able or willing to pay the full fee, it was accepted by the caseworker at the end of the interview. It sometimes proved awkward for the caseworker to raise the question of the fee.

Caseworker: I have a more or less gentle way of saying 'Did you have time to receive our brochure?' and if they say no, then I hand them one. During the interview or perhaps at the end of the interview, I'll say something about, "You know there is a counselling fee, a consultation fee?"
Evaluator: "Would you rather that this was handled separately?"
Caseworker: "Well, that was one of the problems in the beginning. I feel that it is not handled very gracefully at the present time. I don't like the situation of bringing a woman to a discussion of a fee after she has really had a kind of an emotional experience."
Second caseworker: "I feel it is very difficult for us to bargain with a woman. This is difficult for me. It always has been. I would like to have it just the way you go to a psychiatrist. The fee is expected."
Third caseworker: "Well, I am accustomed to setting a fee. This is part of the caseworker's responsibility. Most agencies do have a sliding fee scale and you open this to discussion. But I must say, this has to come at the end, very often, of a very long interview . . . The person is often emotionally spent, and perhaps that is part of the reason why short shrift is made of this fee thing. I cannot go into extreme detail, so that I have to make approximations and attempt to work with the client around the fee. I don't want a fee to be a deterrent to someone seeking help, and at the same time I don't want it to be used as a form of manipulation. You have to constantly assess it and allow the person to know that the fee is open to reassessment."

The fees for the group discussions, legal discussions, and financial consultations were set on the same $12.50 or less sliding scale. Actually, most clients paid much less. During the month of January 1972 the Center had one hundred and ten individual casework interviews, twenty-nine group discussion client visits, and seven financial consultations, for a total of 146 sessions for which a fee was asked. Total income from fees that month was $560.00. This means that the average fee collected was only $3.80.

The reactions of clients to the fees were assessed in the follow-up interviews. The clients were asked whether they had paid a fee; if so, how much; and whether they thought this was too much, too little or a fair amount.

Those widows who felt that the fees they paid were fair or too little generally paid little or no fee. Many of them had adequate income or assets and felt that the Center had helped them. Nevertheless, their idea of what the service of the Center was worth tended to be much less than would be necessary to pay the actual costs incurred. Some typical comments illustrate this problem:

A woman who had paid $3.50 said, "I was sorry I couldn't pay the full amount. It was fair."
One who paid $1.00 commented, "This is too little, considering the service, but it's what I can afford now."
A client who had paid $5.00 for the first visit and nothing for the two group sessions she had attended said, "Since it was just for the first visit, it was O. K."
A woman who had sizable assets in savings and investments said, "I paid $7.50 because on the radio that was the charge they mentioned. $12.50 seemed a little too much for the type of advice they gave."

The fee thus remains a problem for the Center, because it is somewhat awkward to collect, may deter some widows from coming, and yet generates very little revenue compared to the costs of running the services. Many widows cannot afford anything more than a token fee. Others who would not blanch at paying $25 or so for a full hour's physical examination from a medical doctor seem to feel that consultation by a professional for emotional or other personal problems should not cost even half that much. Any agency which provides individual casework consultations for widows is therefore going to have to rely on fairly large subsidies or grants to pay its expenses rather than generate most of its income from client fees.

5

THE CLIENTS AND THEIR PROBLEMS

In this chapter, we will first take an overall look at the nature and extent of the problems of the widows who have been clients at the Center
and at their socio-economic characteristics. Then we will look at the most
frequently encountered problems in more detail and see how their incidence
is related to various characteristics of the widows.

The widows who come to the Center for help are by no means representative of all widows in the New York metropolitan area. Compared to
the total population of widows, they are disproportionately likely to be
recently bereaved, white, Jewish, living alone, unemployed, and with slim
financial resources. Their most serious problems are likely to include emotional upsets, finding new friends and activities, managing money, and
finding a job. Even after several years of widowhood, they are likely to
feel that no one cares about or understands them, that there isn't any reason to go on living.

The clients on whom we have case records and follow-up interviews are
the result of self-selection and Center selection. First, the widow had to
become aware of the Center and have the motivation to come and ask for
help. This self-selection process probably means that prospective clients are
more likely to be attuned to the mass media than other widows, more
likely to have serious problems, less likely to have other sources of help
to turn to, and more likely to have a personality structure which enables
them to take the potentially humiliating step of asking for help. Secondly,
the screening of potential clients by the Center eliminated from individual
casework (and thus from this study) many older widows, long-term widows,
and those whose only problems had to do with poverty, old age, or housing,
or whose problems could be dealt with by telephone referral or advice.

Thus, the description of the clients of the Center presented here is that of a particular segment of the widows in our population. However, it is probable that their characteristics and problems are similar to those which would be shared by the clients of services for widows in other communities.

Thus, the characteristics of the Center's clients should be useful to other agencies contemplating establishing services to widows as a rough prediction of the kinds of clients who will come to them, their presenting problems (the problems they first mention to the intake worker), and the needs for help that are most prevalent.

SOCIO-ECONOMIC CHARACTERISTICS OF THE CLIENTS

The characteristics of clients as described in this section come from the case history records of the 437 widows who received at least one individual consultation during the first few years of the Center's operation covered by the evaluation project.

Most the clients were recently bereaved. Twenty-eight percent had lost their husband less than a year before, and 32% had been widowed for from one to three years before the first consultation. However, this leaves slightly over a third who had been widowed for more than three years, including 15% of all clients who had been widowed for eleven years or more before coming for help. Thus the majority of clients for services aimed at widows will be recent widows, but a significant number will be long-term widows, whose problems are not likely to be amenable to any structured group treatment program. A program aimed only at dealing with the recently bereaved in the throes of acute grief would have disqualified a very large proportion of the widows who came to the Center for help.

Table 5.1 summarizes the most relevant socio-economic characteristics of the clients. In terms of age, more than a quarter are over sixty-five, and practically none are under forty-five. This indicates that for a large proportion of the clients, the problems of widowhood are superimposed on the general problems of old age. An agency that arbitrarily limited itself to serving younger widows—say, under fifty-five—would exclude most potential clients who wanted help and were judged by the Center screening process as likely to benefit from individual counselling.

In terms of religion and race, the clients are not representative of the population of widows in the metropolitan area. Over half of the clients are Jewish, and only 8% are black. Asked why this happened, one caseworker explained:

Caseworker: I don't know why this is, other than that those who seek what is even quasi-private help tend to be Jewish people. They utilize all

Table 5.1

Socio-economic Characteristics of 477 Clients.

Age		Religion		Number of persons living with widow		Education		Yearly income of widow		For those answering insurance on husband		Amount of life insurance on husband	
Under 45	9%	Protestant	11%	None	58%	Less than high school	26%	Under $3,000	27%	None	43%	None	27%
45-54	25%	Catholic	22%	One	20%	High school graduate	44%	$3,000-$4,999	18%	Less than $1,000	29%	Less than $1,000	16%
55-64	33%	Jewish	52%	Two or more	15%	Higher education	17%	$5,000-7,499	11%	$1,000-$9,999	17%	$1,000-$9,999	17%
65 and over	28%	Other	3%	No answer	7%	No answer	13%	$7,500 and over	7%	$10,000 and over	11%	$10,000 and over	10%
No answer	5%	None	4%	No answer	8%			No answer	37%	No answer		No answer	30%

Source: Case history records of 477 widows.

varieties of services much more than other groups do. They see a need for help and they have no compunction about asking for help, is my feeling. I have several black and Puerto Rican clients, and have begun to fit them into our social groups, despite the minority that they are in. Perhaps as we get more, they will feel nonthreatened in this kind of environment.
Evaluator: You don't have any feelings about how—
Caseworker: How one would go about getting more? Well, I guess the usual channel is various black groups and the black press. Certainly *El Diario* for the Puerto Rican population. But if your philosophy remains the same, that you are not set up for poverty, then you are letting yourself open for a greater proportion of clients with poverty problems.

Only a third have a child living with them at home, and 58% report that there is no one at all living with them. This points up the social isolation of a majority of the clients.

Only 31% of the widows were employed either part-time or full-time when they came to the Center. Another 26% were unemployed and either actively seeking a job or open to employment if a suitable job should turn up. Those who are employed tend to be in clerical, retail sales, and other lower white-collar jobs. Related to this is the fact that they typically are high school graduates. However, over a quarter have not finished high school, and this, combined with the fact that they are likely to be over fifty-five, makes it nearly impossible for them to find a well-paying job.

Financially, the situation is bleak for most of the widows. Only one out of ten reports that there was any substantial amount of life insurance on the husband. If the husband was collecting a pension, the likelihood is that the pension ended with his death. If they are collecting social security as survivors, they receive only 80% of the already inadequate amount they were entitled to before the husband's death. We have already seen that age and educational limitations restrict the possibilities for employment for many. The result is that most clients of the Center are living below or near the poverty level for the metropolitan area. This is so in spite of the screening out of widows whose problems are solely those of old age and poverty. These figures point out the failure of a private insurance system and of the society to make adequate financial provision for the typical woman in the last stage of her life—for the typical woman will be a widow, and will become a widow after the age of sixty.

The situation is difficult to change, because traditionally people are most interested in life insurance protection when they are young, when they have young children and the rates are cheap. Insurance owners are increasingly likely to let their policies lapse or cash them in from middle age onward, yet this is precisely when they are most likely to die, leaving their wives with little to live on for the last ten or twenty years of their lives.

THE PROBLEMS FOR WHICH HELP IS NEEDED

There were three different sources of information about the problems of the clients, and the conclusions about the prevalence of various types of problems among the clients depend on which source one examines. First of all, at the time the client initially came to the Center for an interview, she filled out a card at the reception desk giving her name, date of birth, date of husband's death, and "request," or what kind of help she was asking for. This is the problem with which the caseworker generally began (see Table 5.2).

Table 5.2

Initial Requests of 462 Widows Coming to the Center

Request	%
General	21
Find a job	19
Emotional problems	16
Housing	11
Problems with children	8
Government agencies	6
Managing finances	5
Leisure activities	5
Lawyer	3
New friends	3
Other	11
No request (blank or refused to fill out card)	5

Source: Requests given to receptionist and listed on intake cards. Up to two requests were coded. N = 462.

General requests headed the list, and these were of two types. The first was a specifically open-ended request on the part of the widow for restructuring her life. Examples of these are: "The future. Where do I go from here?" "Help in planning my future." "Advice and information." If the widow listed several different problem areas on the request card, this was also coded as general. Examples of these are "possible relocation, vocational guidance, help with depression, and loneliness," and "employment, living conditions, health, finances."

Finding a job is the most frequently listed specific request, followed by emotional problems and then housing. The caseworkers feel, however, that these figures overrepresent the relative prevalence and severity of such specific areas as jobs and housing, because these are presenting problems which are easy to write down in a tiny space and in an impersonal situation. More personal and complex problems, such as emotional problems and problems with children or lack of friends, are not likely to be given in such a situation, but rather to come out only when a sense of trust and rapport has developed between a client and a caseworker or interviewer. These initial requests are thus not a very valid indicator of the extent or relative frequency of the various kinds of problems a widow may have. They are, however, a good indicator of the presenting problems with which such an agency will be asked to deal.

A second source of data on problems is the case history filled out by the social worker following the first long, client-centered interview. In the consultation session, the social worker keeps the case history form in mind as a kind of interview guide and tries to touch on each of the possible problem areas included there to see if it is of concern to the widow. Table 5.3 shows the results of this process. Many more clients report problems of various sorts or are considered to have them by the caseworker than originally list them in their request. For example, help with emotional problems is specifically requested by only 16% of clients filling out their interview request card, but half of all clients are judged to be emotionally disturbed or still suffering from bereavement by the caseworkers who interview them. Whereas 19% asked for help with a job, 40% were found to be interested in finding a job during the course of the interview.

But these data may often be invalid, too. First of all, since the casework intake interview included no structured questions and no specific sequence of topics, many potential problem areas were sometimes not discussed, whether because of limited time or the caseworker's perhaps incorrect assumption that something was not a problem or that the client would not be willing to talk about it at that time. Table 5.3 shows that the case histories contain no record of whether many of these potential problem areas were raised at all during the course of the interview. Secondly, these data were perceptions and judgments by the caseworker about her client's problems, rather than the widow's own feelings about whether she had such problems or not. However, examination of the problems mentioned in the case history-intake interview records may indicate how frequently case-workers in such programs will encounter these problems.

Our final source of data on the frequency and severity of various kinds of problems among widowed clients is the follow-up interview, which included structured questions about each of the main problem areas and recorded the widow's own feelings about whether or not they were problems

Table 5.3

Percentage of 462 Widows Who Mentioned Problems During Intake Interview, and Percentage with Whom Problem Was Not Discussed

	% mentioning problem	% not discussed
Emotional state not balanced	50	5
Health	45	5
Living alone	47	17
Change housing	30	11
Looking for employment	40	13
Relations with children	21	9
Problems with in-laws	12	24
Problems with other relatives	11	38
Relations with old friends	23	20
Finding new friends	34	22
Relations with men	14	23
Settling estate	9	15
Poverty	11	13
Financial management	18	19
Volunteer position desired	8	54

Source: 462 intake interviews. Checklist filled out by caseworker after the interview.

for her when she came to the Center and at the time of the follow-up (see Table 5.4). Comparing the case records with the follow-up interviews, we notice two things. First, the number of widows who reported that they had problems of various types tends to be somewhat larger than the number of those who were reported to have such problems by the caseworker. For instance, while 40% of the clients were found to be looking for a job by the caseworker, 49% of those who completed the follow-up interview said that this had been a "serious" problem or "somewhat of a problem" for them when they came to the Center. But the relative proportions of clients with problems of various types was about the same, whether based on caseworker assessment or self-reporting. Emotional problems head the list, by far. Relations with friends and family and problems in finding a new job or new

Table 5.4

Self-Reporting of Problems by Widows

Problem area	Problem when came to center	Problem now	Number answering
Emotional upset	80%	68%	174
Relations with family	39%	32%	221
Finding a job	49%	39%	230
Living quarters	32%	31%	227
Friends	53%	49%	220
Government agencies	19%	15%	222
Managing money	68%	51%	218
Relations with men	30%	44%	146

Source: Structured questions in response to follow-up interviews.

living arrangements follow and are problems for at least a third of the widows. Large discrepancies do occur in the financial area and in relationships with males, however. Whereas less than a third of the clients were reported by the caseworker to have financial problems of any type, 68% of the widows themselves said they had such problems. And whereas relations with men were reported as a problem area in only 14% of the case histories, 30% of the widows say it was a problem when they talked to the interviewer.

The reason for these discrepancies seems to be that the caseworkers considered these two potential problem areas as ones in which probing could potentially destroy their rapport with the client, and they avoided them if they did not feel sure that the client trusted them. In the follow-up interview, these areas were covered for all those who had a personal interview.

Having examined the overall frequency with which problems of various types were reported by the widows who came to the Center, we will now turn to a more detailed description of the main problem areas, including a look at the relationship between the socio-economic characteristics of the widow and the problems she is likely to have. This more detailed exploration of specific problem areas will be from the point of view of the clients themselves, based on their comments to the caseworkers and follow-up interviewers.

EMOTIONAL PROBLEMS

We have said that emotional problems connected with bereavement are likely to be present for the great majority of the clients of the Center. These become complexly intertwined with more "concrete" problems, financial and social. There is, of course, the direct emotional disturbance of bereavement and grief. In addition, however, the concrete problems of disturbance and dissolution of the widow's main social relationships and removal of the main source of income require many adjustments (finding new friends and activities; finding a job and/or less expensive housing; making a major budgeting effort, etc.). Any major change in role relationships and living patterns is stressful and causes emotional disturbance, but many changes in one's life circumstances and behavior patterns imposed at the same time are especially likely to be associated with extreme stress and such symptoms as mental illness, heart attacks, and suicide.

The emotional stress caused by bereavement, social isolation, and forced changes in life circumstances begin to become entwined in a pathological spiral for many widows if someone does not intervene. Figure 5.1 is an attempt to diagram this conceptualized process. Emotional stress means that people are not likely to be able to sustain good personal relationships, which means that they lose their sources of both emotional support and advice and help for solving their problems. Social isolation and unsolved or poorly solved problems cause more emotional upset. . . causing more inability to take steps that will solve the problems . . . and so on.

The caseworkers are aware of this interdependence of emotional problems with the problems of readjustment of the widow. One of the caseworkers explained that she thought that the emotional problems are *primary*

Figure 5.1

INTERRELATIONSHIP OF PROBLEMS OF WIDOWHOOD

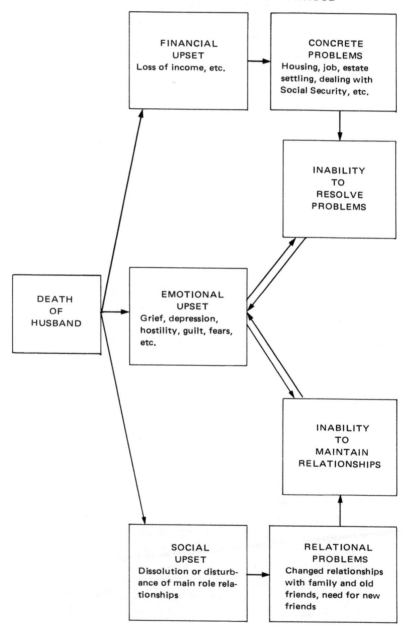

problems, practically speaking, because if these can be resolved, then the widow will be able to take whatever steps are necessary to resolve her more concrete problems:

Evaluator: So you feel that the emotional problems are almost always primary?
Caseworker: The psychological, which is both the ability to think and concentrate, and to recognize the feelings that have to be reintegrated in a way that allows them to reach out to others again. Remember that for the most part the bereaved person shrinks into herself. She needs to live through the whole process of separation and loss, and with it comes a shrinking away of other connections. You have to be aware of what each individual widow needs to regain her sense of balance and move forward into being social again.

What exactly do we mean by "emotional upset"? Here is how some of the widows who say they had serious emotional problems connected with bereavement at the time they came to the Center described their feelings:

"Now suddenly there is nothing . . . I haven't any pleasure from life now . . . I get only $136/month from Social Security and my daughter is supporting me . . . [weeping] He was a brother, teacher, everything to me. I blame myself for not being aware of his problems on his job the last year . . . I was never alone before. This is the first time in my life . . . I'm afraid of every shadow at night . . . I can't eat by myself. I can't sleep. I'm obsessed with making sure the door is closed and the gas oven is off . . . I'm so tired and I can't breathe . . . I can't go for a job. How can I go when I'm afraid even in my own home?" [widowed eight months].
"I couldn't function at all. My thinking was very poor. I couldn't absorb or retain reading a newspaper or watching TV. I had lost over twenty lbs. I couldn't sleep nights. I couldn't eat . . . I can't stand this house. It's like a compulsion to get out. I've had terrible fears . . . I'm very insecure and afraid of changes" [widowed sixteen months].
"I felt very lonely, not able to accept or cope with my situation."
"I'm so frightened and so alone. I escape in sleep. The present frightens me, and the future, more."
"The whole problem is . . . [crying], I can't forget my husband. It was very hard . . . Sometimes I'm by myself and I just cry and cry."
"I was very, very bad. I cried. If I didn't have a strong belief in God I would have cracked up. Being proud I never cried in public, but in the house, what those four walls have heard! I cried, I screamed . . . I adored him. Ours was the perfect marriage . . . Life can never be the same without him . . . I miss him most when I come in at 4:30 and he's not there" [widowed five years].

Here is an account of a "typical" problem, detailing a troubled emotional state and its intertwining with family and other problems, as described by a caseworker in a case history. (The client had been widowed nine years, it should be noted, and was in much worse emotional condition than she had been earlier in her widowhood):

The applicant appears to be suffering from a combination of guilt feelings, bitterness, resentment, confusion and what she describes as a sense of emptiness, hopelessness, and complete inability to cope with either practical problems or her emotional distress. At the same time, she was able to mobilize herself to the extent of calling for an appointment and coming to this office for an interview. From the material reported, she is adequately prepared in training and experience to pursue her profession but so emotionally depleted that she has no wish to resume work. She recognizes, however, that this is essential from a practical as well as therapeutic viewpoint. Although she claims to have broken off relationships with friends, family, and professional associates, this is not altogether true since references to contacts indicate the opposite . . . Their many friends in this country and abroad were sympathetic and considerate but after awhile these contacts fell off. Applicant has been deteriorating both professionally and in her personal life. Her present distress is centered mainly on the alienation of her daughter . . . The applicant wept from time to time throughout the interview mainly in self-pity when speaking of her husband's failure to relate to her in a meaningful way and of her daughter's cruelty. She describes an occasion some weeks ago when she had recently returned from the hospital, was recovering from her coronary attack, and was under sedation. Her daughter came to her room in the early hours of the morning and began questioning her about her life with (the deceased), about his extra-marital affairs as well as applicant's intimacies with other men. Applicant feels that the daughter took advantage of her weakened condition to extract information and to torture her with probing questions . . . Applicant is suffering from a great deal of guilt toward her daughter and admits that throughout the child's life she gave her very little time or attention.

One might consider the above sort of situation a kind of "chronic" one, and a crisis reached soon after the death of the husband as an "acute" situation.

A caseworker described the emotional problems of many of the recent widows she counselled like this:

You must understand the kind of crisis that these women are in. In the first state of shock and depression you do not have to worry about suicide. They are numb, in a shell, But when the numbness begins to wear off and they finally understand that the husband is really gone—that he will never be back and that their whole life is changed—that is when they get depressed, sometimes to the point of suicide or homicide. The pain is too much, they do not want to live. They see reminders everywhere. His clothes come back from the cleaners. In all the closets and drawers there are reminders of him, material things that have outlived him. Every time she sees them there is terrible suffering. She comes home and she sees the image of her husband when she opens the door, lying there in rigor mortis. She cannot get this terrible image out of her mind. Her whole life has changed, and every change is acutely painful. If she refuses to change, to accept and adjust, she becomes mentally ill. You have got to work on her to get her to accept it. She will come through as long as there is someone there. If she becomes aware of loneliness she begins to feel that she is important to no one, that there is nothing to live for.

According to the case histories recorded by the caseworkers, the following proportions of clients demonstrated various symptoms of emotional problems during the intake interview. Thirty-one percent cried (rising to 48% of those widowed less than one year); 53% mentioned loneliness (rising to 70% of recent widows); 44% expressed feelings of anxiety and/or nervousness. No other expressions of bereavement-related emotions were very frequent overall, although among clients widowed less than one year, feelings of hostility, anger, or blame toward others in relation to the husband's death were expressed by 17%; 12% expressed feelings of guilt about not having treated their husband better; and 9% expressed feelings of bitterness and unfairness about the death ("Why me? Why not X, instead?").

The follow-up interviews, which were conducted in person, systematically covered several kinds of bereavement symptoms, and these self-reports also indicate that large proportions of the widows who were clients of the Center had serious emotional problems related to the death of their husband, even years after they had become widowed.

The information on emotions related to bereavement or recovery was obtained at the very end of the personal interview, when the interviewer hoped to have established a good relationship with the widow. The statements and the responses are shown in Table 5.5. (In these tabulations, those who said "yes" or some other reply which did not fit into one of the three categories offered are included in "occasionally.") There is not as much improvement in the emotional state of the widow with the passage of time as might be expected, at least for the widows who came to the Center, as shown in Table 5.6. (This table combines the "most of the time" and "occasionally" replies as the proportion reporting the feelings.) The small number of cases in many of the cells of the table accounts for some of the fluctuations in percentages, but a pattern is discernible. Not only had the emotional problems of clients who had been widowed from four to ten years not subsided: these widows were more emotionally troubled than the clients widowed more recently, at least by the indicator that over half felt at least occasionally that there is no reason for them to go on living. The mere passage of time does not guarantee recovery. Feelings of total isolation, as indicated by "nobody cares about me" and "nobody understands how I feel," still characterize about half of the clients who have been widowed over ten years. Although guilt decreases, insomnia plagues over half of the long-term widows, and more than a quarter are so emotionally unstable that they are afraid they might have a nervous breakdown. In other words, the detailed questions we asked support the widows' own judgments that many of them have quite serious emotional problems related to their widowhood.

Table 5.5

Responses to Questions about Bereavement Symptoms

Symptoms	% Not at all	% Occa- sion- ally	% Most of the time	Total (exclud- ing no response)
Nobody cares about me.	53	32	15	100
No one really understands how I feel.	59	26	25	100
I feel somehow it was my fault that my husband died.	82	12	6	100
I can't seem to sleep. I lie awake for hours after I go to bed.	39	28	33	100
There doesn't seem to be any reason to go on living.	51	32	17	100
I'm worried I might have a nervous breakdown.	73	16	12	100
I'm going to be able to work things out.	44	30	27	100
I am finding some new meanings and purposes in life.	44	30	27	100

Note: The statements were introduced as follows: "I am going to read you some statements that many widows have made. I would like you to tell me how often in the last month you have had thoughts or experiences like these: not at all, occasional-ly, or most of the time."

Source: Follow-up interviews; N = 135.

Table 5.6

Percentage of Widows Reporting Feelings Related to Poor Emotional Adjustment

Statement	Years widowed at time of interview			
	% less than 3	% 4-10	% 11+	% of all widows
Nobody cares about me.	46	46	47	47
No one really understands how I feel.	58	46	47	51
I feel somehow it was my fault that my husband died.	25	10	7	18
I can't seem to sleep.	63	61	53	61
There doesn't seem to be any reason to go on living.	48	56	40	49
I am worried I might have a nervous breakdown.	25	34	27	27
I am going to be able to work things out (% who responded "not at all").	13	22	7	15
I am finding some new meanings and purposes in life (% who responded "not at all").	44	51	27	44

Source: 135 personal follow-up interviews.

FAMILY PROBLEMS

Children are by far the most likely family members to generate problems for the widow. Altogether, 31% of widows mentioned a problem with a child (16% sons, 15% daughters). Eight percent of widows reported problems with in-laws; 6% with siblings (5% sisters, 1% brothers). All other types of relatives (parents, grandparents, etc.) presented problems for only 4% of the clients. In the figures reported, it should be noted that two sources of family conflict were coded for some of the clients.

How many of these relational problems existed before the death of the husband and father, and how many developed or seriously worsened due to his absence, we do not know. The specific types of problems are as varied as the possible patterns of interaction, and we failed to ask a question such as "Did this problem exist before the death of your husband?" We coded up to two family problems for each widow. Altogether, we found 17% complaining of coldness, unfriendliness, or similar behavior by family members. Fifteen percent were having difficulties with children who were misbehaving or had developed problems of their own. We also had 21% of clients reporting assorted other family problems which seemed to form no identifiable clusters.

The coldness or unfriendliness reported again and again involved perceived neglect or failure to give the widow as much attention and assistance as she thought she ought to get. Especially with children, the isolated widow often seems to have had her expectations disappointed, as can be seen from some of the accounts of family problems which follow.

"I was the youngest in my family and now they are all dead. My two daughters are the only ones I have. I could not expect any sympathy from them. They were concerned with themselves."

"I was surprised. I would have expected more support from my own family. My sister seemed a little cold and indifferent. My mother and father are still alive, and I expected more emotional support from them."

"After my husband died, I'd go once a week to help my daughter with her baby. But it didn't have to be just Fridays as it was. She could have invited me over more. She could have told me just to drop in, which she didn't, so now [crying] my daughter lets two weeks pass by without seeing me, calls me only every three or four days instead of every day. I could be dead, I could go blind at any moment, and she knows that."

"I am lonely. I have two sons but they are both married. One is a doctor; he calls me but he is busy. The other son is working during the day and goes to school at night. So his time is taken up. They have their own problems."

The other main type of problems with relatives centers around various types of perceived misbehavior or failure by the children, sometimes including serious defiance such as taking drugs, other times involving hostility toward the mother and/or a total breakdown in communications.

"My son is going with a married woman who has a child, and I'm unhappy about that."

"My nineteen-year-old son is not working. He is unhappy and he gets at me. I worry because he has no money, what trouble will he get into. He bugs me and I yell at him."

"My son is unemployed. I want him to make a living. I would like him to get married. He's too quiet, not aggressive enough. Now he's just disgusted and it makes me sick."

"My son is twenty-one. I am afraid he is taking drugs, marijuana and maybe pills. He hasn't worked for a year. He comes home at all hours of the night bringing his friends with him. Then he is very defensive and very disrespectful. Only last week he came in at 1 A.M. with a friend and I got so mad I called the police to put the friend out."

"My son is going to be nineteen. He lives here but never speaks to me. He locks his room door and won't eat anything I make for him."

LACK OF FRIENDS AND LEISURE ACTIVITIES

For almost all wives, social and recreation activities are couple-based. Though she may talk quite a bit with a neighboring wife, for instance, the two couples may also play bridge together and the two men may play golf together. With the death of the husband, the woman no longer fits in with her old friends and their couple-based round of activities. The loss of old friends is of course even more complete if she moves. This theme occurs again and again, as shown in the variations below:

"I have never felt normal—never felt either fish or fowl—never was comfortable with couples or with widows alone or with anyone since I was widowed."

"I find it difficult going out. I'm a fifth wheel . . . old friends don't seem close anymore. It's difficult to make new friends. I always thought there was nothing so pathetic as a bunch of lonely widows."

"After your husband goes, friends are no longer yours. They know you're lonesome and wonder whose husband you are going after . . . Where can a woman go? There's a million bars around here, but you can't go alone, not even to a nice restaurant."

"Just as soon as you have no mate, you are dropped. It is just as if you have leprosy."

"My husband and I needed no one. We had each other . . . [now] I don't have any close friends, someone I could confide in. I have friends who call once in a while . . . they take you out to dinner but you feel like a third cog."

"Couples can no longer include you . . . I try to do things to make it easier for people to have me with them. I'm not a complainer. It's never too hot, too cold, too far or anything like that."

Note that a feeling of stigma, of being a misfit and a burden if they "impose" themselves on others, emerges through these accounts. Widows feel that they are defined by others as pathetic and undesirable to have around and sometimes as a sexual threat. This, of course, tends to cut down on their attempts to make new friends because they feel nobody would want them. If they are over sixty-five, then the stigma of age in our society compounds the stigma of being a woman without a partner of her own.

The result is that many widows have few friends and few leisure activities that provide them with either social interaction or exercise or mental stimulation. When asked what they do with their time many give answers such as these:

"I watch TV. I sometimes go to a neighbor when I feel like it. Maybe once or twice a week, but not on weekends because their husbands are home . . . I just don't go anyplace. I can't afford it anyway."

"I find I'm left out of things now. I have no partner . . . I devote my time to the children, watch TV with them, clean the house."

A coding of the leisure activities mentioned, with up to three reported activities included for each widow, resulted in 8% claiming they had no leisure activities at all. Television, reading, and other solitary passive activity were reported by 37%, and sewing, knitting, or other solitary hobbies by 16%. Thirty-four percent said they spent some time visiting with friends and relatives; movies, plays, museums, etc., were mentioned by 12%. Cards, club meetings, or other social recreation were reported by 21%, and sports or exercise activities by only 8%.

At least a quarter of the widows who came to the Center were almost completely isolated from frequent, meaningful social relationships, as indicated by their answers to questions on how many people they had visited within the preceding week, and how many friends they had. One quarter reported not a single visit with anyone during the preceding week, 12% had visited with only one person, 47% had seen two or more people, and 15% did not answer the question. As for close friends, 23% said they had none at all, 22% had only one or two, 41% reported three or more, and 13% would give no information about whether or not they had any close friends.

MALE COMPANIONSHIP

This problem obviously overlaps with the preceding section on friends and leisure activities. Without a male, widows are excluded from couple-based activities, and without an escort to give them a sense of security, they often feel afraid to go anywhere alone at night.

The typical client found this an emotion-charged subject. For these women, one does not just have friends, some of whom happen to be male, as one could have friends, some of whom were younger or older or different in another way. During the first year or so, while active mourning is still going on, thoughts or mention of men seem to be considered disloyal or improper by most widows.

Later, a male friend often comes to symbolize "the answer"; if only I had a man who married me, then I'd have someone to *take care* of me, and I wouldn't have to worry about supporting myself or raising fatherless children or being friendless, etc., etc. Many widows want very badly to re-establish a dependent relationship with a replacement for their dead husband. At the same time, they are very wary of being exploited by the man they hope to attract into marriage and frequently express extreme distaste or fear about sexual relationships. Some of these themes come out in the quotations below from the follow-up interviews:

"If you had a good relationship beforehand you miss it now . . . I'd like to find the carbon copy of my husband."

"I would like to meet somebody. I need somebody to take care of me and support me."

"If there was a man in the house things might be different. A man is strong and might help the situation with my son."

However, fears about relationships with men were expressed at least as frequently:

"No, I haven't done any dating at all. I would have, but it's hard to meet men . . . You're fearful when you're widowed. You know what you had, not what you may get."

"I would like male companionship—I'd like to get married again. The thought of sex with anyone except my husband 'turns me off'. But I *would* like a companion, and I suppose *'that'* would follow."

"I don't like to go out. I loved my husband too much. I would like to be in the company of a man, but not to date . . . If I do meet someone, I get cold feet."

"It would be nice to have an escort . . . I'm not a sexy woman . . . If I got married I suppose *that* would have to be part of it."

EMPLOYMENT

Many problems, such as finding a job, not having enough money, or needing new living quarters, are self-evident. We will look at the employment problem in some detail, however. The widow needs a job since she has lost her main source of financial support, and she also needs a job to give herself a new life routine, social contacts, and self-identity to fill the void. For many widows, getting a good job is seen as the key to solving most of their other problems. As one widow put it:

If I had a better job [than part-time typing], I'd have more money, I wouldn't be living here, I'd have more of a social life. I'd have no problems. Everything hinges on one thing, all the others would just follow.

However, the widow who comes to the Center is likely to have been a housewife most of her life and to have no skills that command a decent salary in the marketplace. Nervousness at being put in the unaccustomed position of looking for a job may add to the already serious liabilities she has in this regard:

"I'd like to work but they don't offer me anything. I fill out applications and that's as far as it goes."

"I have no training and I was out of work for a long time. I used to help my husband at his business, until he retired."

"I needed a job desperately . . . They sent me to an agency where they wanted to give me a test. I got very nervous. I'm not good at math. So I just walked out."

The extent of this problem is partially documented by the fact that at the time they came to the Center, 64% of the clients reported themselves as "housewives" or "unemployed," and only 1% had a professional occupation.

Slightly more than half of the clients (54%) claimed that they did not want a job, however. Of those who were seeking employment, the desperate *"anything"* is the most likely request, or else some kind of clerical or other white collar job. It is interesting to note that whereas only 31% reported employment when they first came to the Center, 48% were working at the time of the follow-up. Thus, despite the difficulties involved, quite a few clients had managed to find jobs. However, of those who were working at the time of the follow-up, almost as many were doing volunteer or part-time work as were working full-time at a paying job.

CHARACTERISTICS ASSOCIATED WITH HAVING VARIOUS PROBLEMS

There is not as strong a relationship as might be expected between socio-economic characteristics and the reporting of serious problems of different types by the widows who came to the Center. This is probably because the widows who did come were not a representative sample of the general population of widows, but rather those who defined themselves as having problems serious enough to require help.

As would be expected, the more recent widows are more likely to have emotional problems related to bereavement. Perceived problems in finding new friends or activities peak in the period of one to three years after the death (see Table 5.7).

In relation to age, family problems are most likely to occur for the younger widows, who have children at home. Problems with finding new friends or activities, male companionship, and managing money are also more likely to be reported by widows under fifty-five. Younger widows are also somewhat more likely to have problems with government agencies,

Table 5.7

Widows Reporting Serious Problems When They Came to the Center

Problem Area	Number of Years Widowed at that Time				
	Less than 1	1-3	4-10	11+	All
Emotional	67%	63%	45%	Not asked	----
Family	18%	25%	24%	24%	23%
Finding a job	26%	30%	31%	17%	27%
Living quarters	10%	18%	18%	33%	18%
Finding friends	25%	44%	26%	14%	31%
Government agencies	17%	9%	9%	14%	12%
Male companionship	9%	13%	11%	6%	10%
Managing money	35%	30%	31%	39%	33%
Total number	61	91	48	30	226

Source: Case histories.

since age alone does not qualify them for benefits such as Social Security.

The only variation associated with religion is that 71% of the Jewish widows report serious emotional problems, compared to 53% of the Protestants and Catholics.

Widows with some college education are somewhat more likely to report emotional problems and problems with missing male companionship or managing money than are less educated women. On the other hand, the widows with less education most frequently report serious problems related to family, friends, and living quarters.

Variations associated with financial security are difficult to assess, because so many widows did not answer the questions on income and savings and also because very few of those who came to the Center have more than very modest resources. One predictable and consistent difference which emerged on analysis of the relationship between income, assets, and types of problems is that women with higher levels of income or savings are not as likely to be looking for a job. (For instance, only 10% with an annual income of $5,000 or more reported "serious" employment-related problems, compared to a third of those with lower incomes.) A more interesting relationship is that those widows who are better off are more likely to report serious emotional problems (75% of those with savings of $10,000 or more, compared to 56% of those with no savings).

6

THE INDIVIDUAL CASEWORK PROCESS

In terms of sheer numbers, the service most frequently given to widows by the Widows Consultation Center is information, advice, or referrals over the telephone. Especially during the winter months when travel is difficult, these telephone consultations can become quite extensive. The magnitude of the job of giving service to clients over the telephone is indicated by the sample records in Table 6.1, which were kept by the receptionists on the requests made by persons who called.

There is also a considerable volume of mail inquiries, which are usually answered with advice about community agencies in the writer's area which might be able to help her, and often some pamphlets or other written material about a problem area she had raised. Records kept during the first year of operation showed 135 written requests and responses.

For those widows whose problems seem unlikely to be appropriately solved by referral or advice over the telephone or by mail, a personal appointment is suggested. The primary means by which the Center tries to help its clients deal with their problems is this individual consultation by a caseworker, with follow-up through subsequent appointments, letters or calls in most cases, plus referral to therapeutic discussion groups or other specialized services offered by the Center, when appropriate.

In this chapter, we will be looking at the casework process through the eyes of the caseworkers themselves, using their descriptions of how they try to deal with the problems their clients have and their feelings about where they have been most helpful. Obviously, this is not a textbook on the nature of the social casework process in general, but rather a look at how graduate-educated psychiatric social workers have adapted their generalized skills to the specific task of helping widows. A subsequent chapter, on the effectiveness of the Center, will evaluate the services from the points of view of the clients.

CASEWORK INTERVIEWS AS A SUPPORTIVE, LONG-TERM PROCESS

During the intake interview, the social worker explores the problems and feelings of the widow. Initially it was assumed that for many clients, one or two such sessions would be the extent of individual consultation. The caseworker would make whatever referrals and suggestions she thought

Table 6.1

Disposition of Telephone Inquiries

	January 1972	June 1972
Service	456	565
Information	322	343
Brochures	237	152
Appointments	102	86
TOTAL	1,117	1,146

Source: Receptionist's records.

might help, including referral to group therapy or specialized consultants at the Center. However, this turned out to be a basic misconception about how the casework process would normally proceed. In talking about how she perceived the length of the casework process necessary in order to help most widows, a caseworker explained:

Except for a very small number of people I have seen, I would say that one or two interviews do not do the trick. Very rarely—maybe some women are well put together, and they want financial advice. That you can handle (in one or two visits). But sometimes underneath that request for financial advice come other things which don't take just one session. It's not that often that you can get something so concrete and circumscribed that you can deal with it on a one shot basis and say that you've done your job well . . . I feel that it is impossible to take a woman who is deeply grieved and say, 'Here, I gave you words of wisdom. Go forth.' I can't play God that way . . .

I think that our idea is that there is no time limit on grieving . . . It's our responsibility to continue to see them—if it's just once a week, every two weeks, or some women like to call in just to let you know that they're still there and to get a little shot in the arm sort of thing. But I can't give you a time limit, this is so individual . . .

Another caseworker described what she tried to do and why this usually requires several visits:

They get an approach here that they can't get elsewhere. An immediate caring about them and whatever their problem is, and my imparting to them my genuine respect for all they have been through in life. If I can have regard for them, it gives them courage that they can make it.

One thing I have had to work with is that none of this can happen in only one or two interviews—it is not possible. It is a life process that has to be reorganized in a way that is right for her. A restoration of a sense of wanting to live and to use yourself better. You can't just put them off and say only one or two interviews. They need someone to lean on and to trust while they take their steps.

When the widow in grief is coming to us, she is taking a step to help herself. She is so lonely, she cannot even sleep. Maybe she puts the radio on at two or three in the morning just to hear the sound of a human voice, and that is when she hears our announcement. This little spurt of effort to help herself, to pull out of her depression, is what we have to pick and hold onto. We have to help her to find the strength to live through it. There *cannot* be another abandonment at this point. I think that the agency did not foresee that bereavement work is necessarily emotional support. You have got to stay with it, to be there when they need someone, as they begin to climb up once again from their depression.

There was some pressure by the sponsors to refer widows with severe emotional problems to outside mental health agencies. (The reasons for this pressure were that there seemed to be other agencies in the community equipped to deal with mental illness, and for the Center to take on this task would be an expensive drain on its resources.) However, the staff of the Center did not feel that it was right to rely on such referrals, given conditions in New York City. As one caseworker explained:

Referral to mental health clinics involves a three-to-six-week waiting period for the initial interview. There is also the problem of cost: $25 to $30 for the diagnostic interview and more for subsequent interviews. Some women cannot afford this.

Some people used to think that if a person talked and threatened suicide, they wouldn't do it. But we know now that they mean it, they cannot be ignored, or told to wait, or it may be too late . . .

As a result of the lack of adequate clinical facilities elsewhere, therefore, clients who are quite severely disturbed or possibly suicidal are seen once or twice a week, plus receiving telephone calls.

The pattern of encouraging several consultations over several weeks or months, rather than seeing a client only once or twice, developed slowly over the first year of operation. We do not have data on the total average number of visits per client, but we do know that the visits per month went up fairly steadily. In January 1971, the average number of visits per client for the month was only 1.06, meaning that practically all of the clients came only once. By November 1971, the cut-off date for follow-up interviews with clients, this average was up to 1.60, and by April 1973, near the end of the pilot program period, the average had reached 1.75 visits per client for the month.

Overall, 77% of clients during the first eighteen months had only one individual consultation, 10% had two consultations, and only 13% of the cases included in this study involved three or more visits.

Most of the early clients did receive some follow-up service, however. Twenty percent of the 447 case history records examined showed one follow-up telephone call by the caseworker to the client and 33% showed two or more such calls. In addition, the caseworkers wrote letters on behalf of 33% of the widows, made telephone calls on behalf of 48%, and in 11% of the cases had a private consultation with a member of the widow's family.

DEALING WITH EMOTIONAL PROBLEMS

What exactly does the caseworker do to try to help a widow work through her grief and overcome her emotional problems? On the basis of their experience with clients, the caseworkers feel that most of the widows who come to them probably have some emotional problems which are bound up with the more concrete problems that they may mention. As a caseworker explains:

Very often the person comes in with a presenting problem, something concrete like, "I need employment." With many, that's unimportant, just the tip of the iceberg. They can't tell you at the beginning that they can't cope with life in general.

The caseworker tries to listen sympathetically and to get the client to express all of her feelings and problems, especially the things she has kept bottled up because her friends and relatives are unwilling to put up with her thoughts of death and despair for more than a short time. As a caseworker explained:

Let me tell you, when the women come in this door and they sit down here, they come through with all of their frustrations and disappointments, and they leave feeling almost as if there was a catharsis. That in itself, even though we have taken up only a few things to help them move on, makes them feel so much better . . .

I enter into a helping process, which means that I give an empathetic acceptance to this woman. The angers, the resentments, the feelings of being abandoned—the usual symptomology of bereavement—if you can accept that so that she doesn't have to struggle to prove it to you, then you can move along much more quickly. She has deposited on you her negative feelings and then is more able to begin to find more positive feelings.

The initial consultations with the caseworker are frequently very emotional, in other words, and boxes of tissues and cups of hot tea are frequently used items, especially when the subject of the husband's death and the widow's feelings about it are discussed. Here is a description of such a discussion, taken from casework records:

Mrs. A. cried brokenly, explaining that she cries only in the privacy of her home, "but you are like a sister, so allow me," and she gulped back her tears. The family, both married daughters and sons-in-law and the four grandchildren, were gathered in the A. home to celebrate the Passover Seder, awaiting Mr. A's return from work. As the hour grew late, Mrs. A. urged them to begin the Seder, that she would wait for Mr. A. Suddenly the police appeared and announced that Mr. A. had been killed by a car in an accident crossing Broadway (N. Y. C.); the traffic light had suddenly changed while Mr. A. was halfway across. His skull was fractured, and he was pronounced dead. Mrs. A. went into total shock; her sons-in-law went to the morgue to identify the corpse. They made all the necessary arrangements and paid for the costs. "To this day I cannot get used to my husband not being here. I keep looking for him." Sadly, her voice trailing, "It will be so for the rest of my life."

This case, it should be noted, is an example of one of the "danger signals" which often is associated with poor adjustment to widowhood, namely no warning at all of the impending death, but rather the traumatic experience of being informed by public authorities.

Here are excerpts from the account of another first visit which revealed a more pathological reaction to the death:

Mrs. B. had called, saying, "My son and daughter recommended me to come to you because I don't know what to do with myself. I want to die. My husband was killed by his doctor. He was sick, locked up in his stomach, and they opened him like butchers and poisoned him until he died." [In the office] Mrs. B. cried in anger and frustration and then shouted as she continued to accuse everyone of murdering and butchering her husband, was even self-accusatory for allowing this to happen. For the last few years Mr. B had been in frail health. He was a quiet, passive man, uncomplaining. Toward the end he complained of intolerable inner pressure in his stomach, was given a G-I series which revealed intestinal obstruction and required immediate hospitalization for surgery. They brought Mr. B. by car to the hospital and Dr. X there performed the first operation, then explained that two more would be required because the colostomy procedures were necessary. Mr. B. objected to wearing the colostomy bag and refused to undergo two more operations. Therefore, after three weeks recuperation, the doctor agreed to only one more, more intensive operation to be done. "He was already poisoned and the medicines did not cure him," Mrs. B shouted hysterically. Mr. B. underwent the surgery, was found toxemic, was returned to his room where, unattended, he fell from the bed; two days later he succumbed. Mrs. B., crying bitterly, showed me the death certificate—myocardiac infarction, toxemia following surgery for obstruction of intestine. Beside herself with grief and anger, evidently quite incoherent and unable to function for the time, her daughter and son-in-law arranged for the funeral and burial. Mrs. B. accuses them, as well as the doctors, the hospital and the nurses, of having perpetrated Mr. B's murder and in her paranoid obsessions she wants them all brought to justice and punished. She curses her daughter and son-in-law when she visits at their home, that they also be butchered to death like her husband was. She herself feels guilty that she had ever entrusted him to anyone and that she had not done more for him. She comes to us asking WCC to provide her with the necessary lawyer for litigation against them all . . . As we discussed the situation, accepting her extreme feelings and recognizing the anguish, frustration and bitterness that prompted them, she was able to regain some balance, and could present her relationship with her daughter and son-in-law in more wholly balanced terms . . . I further considered with Mrs. B., that if she still wished to bring suit against them, she would have to have proof of some act of negligence or purposeful mistreatment, and she admits that she has none, except that Mr. B. had fallen from the bed . . . Mrs. B. cried, much of the hysteria and bitterness was gone and her sobbing was more mourning and grieving. She seemed more at peace with herself as she dried her face and nodded, "Somehow when you explain it, I know it is all true. I see it is really no use to go to a lawyer."

Many of the widows have had emotional problems before their husband died. As a caseworker put it:

There's no question that we get a tremendous number of people who are severely disturbed, with the disturbance of bereavement superimposed on an already disturbed personality. In addition, many of the clients come several years after the death of their husbands, long after what would be considered the "normal" period of bereavement. They have not made the "normal" recovery and often some event has reactivated their severe depression. For instance, when a widow's children leave home, she may feel terribly depressed and alone. In these cases, the emotional problems may be so "deep" that it takes a long time to sort them out and to make progress.

Listening, accepting, simply being *there* at the other end of the telephone or subway line when there is an emotional crisis: these simple-sounding but time-consuming types of support are thus the main kind of help the caseworkers try to offer to widows with emotional problems. With several visits the hope is that the negative feelings will all come out, and the widow can be encouraged to take steps to improve her life.

Some independent evidence that such nondirective emotional support does form the core of casework comes from follow-up interviews with the clients. As will be seen in a subsequent discussion of the results of these interviews, the widows were most likely to report "just listening" or "just being there when I needed someone to talk to" as their answer to the question on what the Center had done that was most helpful.

RELATIONSHIPS WITH FAMILY MEMBERS

The case histories record that counselling about family relationships was done for 19% of all widows. As was pointed out earlier, for 11% of all widows a consultation was held with other involved family members in order to help to work out the problems: for the remaining 8%, the problem was discussed only with the widow herself. When asked about the techniques used in counselling about family problems, a caseworker explained:

Where I feel that the family would be receptive to seeing me, without feeling that "She's been complaining about me," and feeling threatened by this situation, I have taken the initiative to be in touch with them—with the permission, always, of the client. Sometimes, you realize that you have a very hostile and abrasive woman—they feel life has dealt them a very mean blow and they hate everybody. Their children, they feel, are most unsupportive. Sometimes, you realize as you speak that this woman is pretty hard to take and you try to work with her to "ease" or "cool" it with them. "If you have something to say, say it to me. These relationships you need very much. I can take your anger." You work in this way with some. Some are very unsophisticated and you have to get down to concrete, day-by-day ways of doing this. Others are very quick.

Most of the time I am seeing the widow and hoping that she will come to understand that she is not unique in experiencing these problems, that most parents feel that their children aren't quite doing enough. Most children are just not aware of the problems that their mother is facing. And, it's not their fault that they do not understand. The woman must be a little more gentle and kindly. It's not that the children don't want to give. They don't know how, sometimes.

This is the most frequent kind of family problem, the widow's feeling that children or other relatives have let her down and aren't as supportive as they should be. The caseworker tries to make the widow feel that she shouldn't expect too much from her children, given the norms in our society. In addition, when feasible, she tries to counsel the other family members on how they can be more supportive.

There are other kinds of problems, however, such as a grown child who doesn't support himself financially, or who is a drug addict or a sex deviate, and who causes the widow much anguish. Sometimes the caseworker gets very involved in intensive counselling and intervention with such problems. One such case involved a woman widowed for eleven years who came asking for help with her grown son who had become increasingly dependent and emotionally disturbed. The case history describes the problem and the time-consuming steps taken by the caseworker:

> The pathologic involvement between this devoted mother and her emotionally dysfunctioning son of 32 has become a dilemma for Mrs. M. He has "holed up" in her living room since the break-up of his marriage, has been employed intermittently, his personality steadily deteriorating. Recently, he has become almost totally immobilized, unable to organize himself to get a job, and presenting severe anti-social behavior. Mrs. M. is frightened and bewildered by this regressive change; he is withdrawn, depressed, uncivil, hostile, suspicious, torments and threatens Mrs. M. She feels unable to go on. She takes refuge in her job, refuses vacations and sick leaves, and would like to fill all her spare time with volunteer work. She wants him out of the home, he refuses to budge, and she is caught by his clinging, pleading dependency on her . . .
>
> I find it difficult for her to really come to terms with her own need to separate from her son, on her own initiative. She is ambivalent, would like a separation that would not leave her worried and guilty for forcing him out. "When he works and earns enough money, he may change. Then I wouldn't have to feel bad if he moves away. After all, I'm still his mother."

A few days later the son called:

> He phoned to protest mother's "erroneous statements." I helped him face the fact that mother can no longer tolerate his behavior and intends to leave him; he will have to be on his own. He insisted that she would never leave him, has told him she wants him home and "promised to give me every comfort." He resisted acknowledging that the situation had changed since then. I considered with him his depleted state and retreat from life; underscored his known positive qualities, intellect, skills, talent, and good job experiences—restoring some sense of self-worth. I wondered whether he has to fail himself now, at 32, in the best years of his life. It may be hard after so long a retreat to pull one's strengths and will together, and find the courage to try for a job. He is worth whatever help we can give him. He replied that he must do this himself; in fact, will go this very afternoon to his old employment agency and get lined up for a job.

Later that day, the mother called:

> I advised of her son's conviction that she would never leave him, and that if she really wants to help him and herself she must confront him with her decision . . . Can she? Right now, yes.

Two days later, when the caseworker called Mrs. M.:

She seemed elated that her son has become activated, goes out for job interviews, left with her at 8:30 this morning with hopes of beginning work today. He is more civil, wants to earn his mother's sympathetic approval. She is surprised and grateful, "How did you do it?" I warned that her optimism may be premature, that it is desirable to support her son's efforts toward work and self-reliance by adhering to the plan for their living apart and to break the dependency.

This is not the end of the story. But enough has been related to show the time-consuming nature of such intervention for the caseworker.

Family problems are also frequently referred to an agency in the widow's own community, especially if it is a long-term problem not directly related to the death of the father, or it involves school problems, in which case the community agency is in a better position to communicate with school officials.

In many cases involving serious behavior problems of children, the caseworker decides that intervention is fruitless and that increased understanding by the widow is the only achievable goal. As one caseworker explains it:

If other family members are genuinely concerned in helping to work out the problem, they will come. If, on the other hand, they have removed themselves from the problems of their mother, then you must work with the widow and place her problems in the perspective of her life experience so that she gains insight into what she may have been doing that contributes to that family problem.

Another caseworker explains such an approach as follows:

I think that the widows have to know that there is a limit to what they can do. We do not try to foster guilt. Very often they feel, "What have I done that my child is such and such?" Sometimes, one has to tell them that you can't be omniscient—you're not the only one involved. There are other influences involved (which affected your child). Where you see that there's a definite link-up you can do it, like (telling the mother) "get off her back." But sometimes there are things beyond her ability to handle, and she only aggravates the situation by becoming too deeply involved. Drug addiction obviously—homosexuality—there is little she can do at this point. Her disappointment in her child can be supported, but you also have to support her inability to do anything."

HELPING THE WIDOW TO FIND NEW FRIENDS AND ACTIVITIES

The caseworker may suggest that the widow join a Center-sponsored social group or come to a program organized by the Center, or she may suggest activities in the community.

The way in which the caseworker deals with loneliness and isolation was explored in detail with one social worker. She explained:

> I think most of the time, we listen. Sometimes this kind of ventilation is cathartic . . .
> Then as they get confidence in your understanding of their problem, little by little you can encourage them to meet new people and to make friends, and we do that. If I know a woman who has a certain personality structure and educational background that I think might be a good companion for another woman that I see, I will suggest that they get together. This very often has proved most successful. It's not something that I would have done earlier in my career, but here, this somehow seems to ring a bell with many women. They are very happy to find someone like this—someone to go to a movie with—nothing gives you joy when you have to do it alone. Most of these women have nothing and nobody. They are in that house alone day after day, with nobody calling and nobody caring. And they have to put on a face for the outside world. Their friends are disgusted already, so they have to smile when they don't feel like smiling. Here they can be themselves, and in this way ventilate sufficiently so that they can face other people.

Some kinds of community activities have worked out well, but others are strongly resisted by the widows. Referrals to "Golden Age" or "Senior Citizen" groups fall in the latter category, because most women will refuse to admit that they are in this low-status category. As a caseworker says, "They can be a hundred, and they don't feel old. They go there and they say 'Oh, those people are so old!' " This is perhaps indicative of the outcast status of the aged in our society, that they do not want to associate with each other. One way of easing the widow into a Golden Age group which has worked in some cases is to get her to volunteer her services at a center.

Volunteer work in places like museums, where there are many people, has worked out well. This does not help with the nights and weekends, but as a caseworker says, "If the day is sufficiently active and they have tomorrow also to consider, then the evening goes by a little better."

The social programs that the Center itself sponsors are also recommended, of course, for any client who does not have many friends or who feels that she doesn't fit in with her old friends anymore.

As far as helping the widow to make new male friends, this has been a very sticky issue for the Center. The caseworkers were asked whether they bring this problem area up, and how they deal with it. In reply, one caseworker said:

> I open the door for them . . . This is one area that they will raise if they feel that they are talking to a woman who is understanding. At first, they say it would be nice if they could just talk to a man. I support this, and try

to help them find avenues where they can get into a heterosexual kind of group. When they begin to date, they come in and tell me about it . . . Mostly, they are in need of renewed male attention, and sexual activity if they are young.

A second caseworker talks about relationships with men, "Only if it is appropriate . . . if they volunteer. I don't press it." If the woman does bring this up, she says:

I suggest that she shouldn't go directly about finding male companionship, but make herself as attractive and as interesting as she can. Take on some kind of involvement that makes her interesting or become part of a group where there might be men. I think that she has a far better chance of finding someone congenial for male companionship that way than if she goes to some place where she is going to sit down and wait for someone to approach her. I have to be realistic. A lot of these women are not that attractive physically.

In other words, the caseworker counsels the widow not to try to go to singles dances or other kinds of matchmaking activities, but to get involved in activities in which meeting men will "just happen" in situations which are less likely to lead to her feeling rejected or being exploited.

DEALING WITH MORE CONCRETE PROBLEMS: JOBS, HOUSING, SOCIAL SECURITY

In addition to offering general emotional support and counselling and advice about how the widow can reintegrate her personality and her social relationships, the caseworker also is likely to make many specific kinds of suggestions and referrals to help the client to work out her various problems. Table 6.2 shows the proportions of clients to whom specific kinds of referrals or advice were given.

Help in finding a job is the most frequent kind of problem a widow is likely to bring to the Center, yet the Center's workers feel somewhat frustrated and inadequate in actually being able to find placements for most of their clients. Given the high unemployment rate in the New York area during the period the Center has operated, they have found that "employment possibilities are extremely scarce for the older woman with no marketable skills and little or no experience."

Occasional jobs do come to the attention of the agency, through direct communication from individuals or organizations wishing to employ mature women, and then direct referrals may be made. Where a regular job is not feasible or possible, other means of earning a living are explored. For instance, a client who wished to open a crafts shop, selling wool and other handicraft supplies, was put in touch with another client skilled in crafts such as knitting, needlepoint, and designing. A second client was helped in establishing a cake-baking business from her apartment.

More frequently, however, no direct kind of job contact can be made, and the woman is referred to an employment agency which is set up to serve people who are likely to be turned away by regular commercial agencies. One agency that has been used in this manner is the Federation Employment and Guidance Service, used for many clients who have been out of

Table 6.2

Percentage of Clients Receiving Advice or Referrals for Concrete Problems

Problem	%
Referred for employment	30
Referred for school or training	7
Help with Social Security, Medicaid, etc.	15
Referred to other agencies or services	40
Advised volunteer work	11
Advised psychiatric counselling	9
Advised to join Center group	34
Help in finding housing	12
Legal referral	12
Referred to book or pamphlet	12

Source: Case histories; N = 437.

the job market for many years but have some typing or other skills. Mature Temps, a commercial agency for temporary workers, has also been used as a referral quite frequently. Often these referrals have not led to a job, however. As one caseworker says:

I haven't found them really all that helpful. What bothers me is that I don't like to send someone on a wild goose chase. I find this can be terribly demoralizing and depressing to a woman who is already upset.

If I send them it's with the understanding that I offer no guarantee that they can be of help. I say please do come back and discuss with me what has transpired, and at that point I pick up the pieces if I have to. To give them absolutely no hope is wrong, but to give them false hope is also wrong.

The caseworker who is felt to be helpful in finding a job by the largest proportion of the clients themselves also tries to do some general job counselling, including discussion of the widow's attributes and skills, and what kinds of jobs they might consider, and help in writing a résumé. She says:

Very often they feel insecure and they can't face a new employer. They have to have a little feeling that they really have something to offer—it's a matter of putting something positive into their thinking . . . I talk about continuing education and job training. For example, perhaps a nursing career if she has been a nurse's aide . . . and generally speaking, if a woman has any clerical skills, I can usually give her a *definite* lead. For example, one particular bank has been very kindly disposed toward hiring women.

Thus, job counselling takes the form of exploring the possibilities with the widow, and of giving her some initial leads, plus hopefully, the impetus to keep looking until she finds a job.

As far as housing goes, one caseworker says that she immediately tells clients that there is really nothing she can do for them. It will take years to get to the top of the waiting lists for low- and middle-income housing developments in the city.

In a few cases, the Center has been able to serve as an intermediary to help two widows to share an apartment which has become too large and expensive for one of them. This is necessarily a limited sort of aid, however, since most women don't want to live with a stranger.

The caseworkers can be of some help in housing problems, however, even if they cannot actually do the legwork to find suitable apartments. They can help the woman to consider carefully all the pros and cons of moving versus staying where she is. A caseworker explains:

I suggest they make no decision of any irrevocable type when they are too emotionally involved with their grief, because they don't think clearly then. The mind isn't functioning accurately under stress. There are too many impulsive or compulsive elements to the grief pattern. I've talked to women who have made mistakes, and they admit it, in deciding something too quickly. I always caution that they should think things through as carefully as they can, unless they are under such great financial pressure that they can't afford to keep the thing [house or apartment] going.

In addition, the caseworker may intervene in problems that a client is having with her landlord.

A related area in which the Center has been of very concrete assistance is in helping its clients to find their way through bureaucratic agencies such as Social Security, Veterans Administration, Medicare, etc., and to a lesser extent, private agencies, such as Blue Cross or a pension plan. Asked why their clients needed the caseworker to intervene and serve as advocate for them, a social worker said:

Not everyone needs it. There are people who may present this as a problem and could very well be mobilized to handle it themselves. Not everyone needs me to take them step by step. The tendency is sometimes to do for someone without allowing them the right to do for themselves, with the support or clarification that you can give them. However, there are some people who are so totally immobilized by widowhood and also have had very little contact outside of their own little house, and don't know what to do and feel thoroughly threatened by it. They do need someone to do a little more than just tell them what to do. Then you get the bright person who finds that they need someone behind them to give them a little more of a clout.

For these clients, the caseworker will telephone and/or write letters on their behalf. Sometimes this gets more attention and action, but sometimes the bureaucrat says, "Tell her to come in." In the case of the widow who has tried and failed or not been satisfied, however, the social worker will stay with the problem until some sort of answer or satisfactory accommodation is made. This can be very time-consuming:

Some of the jargon used in some of the applications is so difficult, that I can sometimes be on the phone a long time. I will not let it rest, I keep saying, "Yes, but how would one answer this and what is your name?" I have had forms that truly I did not understand, and I think that this is a way of discouraging people, and the withdrawn and hesitant person might not know that they should continue to badger.

PROBLEMS IN THE CASEWORK PROCESS

For the social worker, there is the constant problem of allocating her time among the needs of all of her clients. A balance must be struck between the needs of new clients who are waiting to be seen and the needs of ongoing clients, some of whom would like to talk to the caseworker several times a week, if she would permit it. A caseworker explains:

It's naturally a cause of tension because in seeing new clients you give more of yourself. It's more of a challenge to sit down with an individual for the first time and listen to her and talk to her and relate to her. It's a very challenging and sometimes exhausting type of interview because you are working all the time and even when you are listening, you are working. Now, when you have a continuing caseload, you are familiar with the background, you have evaluated the problem and you are working on specific problems.

Usually it is not so demanding. You're obviously trying to make some progress with the individual, to have more knowledge of herself, knowledge of how she can handle her depression, how she can build a new life for herself, new interests, new associations.

A second caseworker commented:

There are times when I feel that I would like to see someone more often, but my caseload doesn't permit it. I wish I could see many of the women more often. They ask me, "Please," and I try very hard to fit them in, but there are other responsibilities as well.

A third caseworker added:

There is so much to do. I tried working at night to write up case histories, but I just could not do it. I do make telephone calls at night . . . Bereaved people are very susceptible to the pull of death . . . They are angry at the doctor, at the hospital, at themselves. That is when they become suicidal. You have got to stay close to them at that point.

A quite different type of problem is the unresponsive widow who does not seem to benefit and move forward as a result of counselling. This is most often the case if the widow is brought in by a relative or friend and does not really want to be helped or admit she had a problem. It is also likely to occur for the older, long-term widow. As a caseworker put it:

There is one area I feel frustrated in—when a lady has been a widow for quite a few years, has deteriorated income, health, and housing, there is so *little* you can do to help them with these problems. A lot of them are emotionally unstable. They have gotten into chronic states of bereavement. It requires an enormous amount of time to lift them a little bit out of despair. They need an ongoing supportive service where they can come and talk. Many aren't right for groups—they want an individual supportive caseworker to listen just to them . . .
As I have developed my therapeutic intervention, I recognize that if a woman comes to me within the first couple of years of her bereavement, usually that is the period when she is most susceptible to moving away from her bereavement or bogging down in it or even regressing.

Thus, there is a need for the caseworker to recognize that some clients, especially long-term widows, are going to have to be phased out of counselling in order to provide time for those who are more responsive. This is done by setting appointments further and further apart and by trying to get the client involved in either a Center therapy group or in some kind of counselling or social group in her own community.

SUMMARY

The individual casework process began as a one- or two-visit inventorying of problems for most clients, with referrals to other services within or outside of the Center for longer-term help in solving the problems. It evolved toward a longer-term counselling relationship for the majority of clients, in which the widow is typically seen several times over the course of a year or even longer. The initial sessions tend to take the form of a nondirective, supportive atmosphere in which the widow can bring her grief and problems out into the open. Counselling and support are offered to help her begin to solve her problems, with telephone or personal contacts continued as long as they seem to help the widow in taking steps to build a new life for herself.

All of the caseworkers feel that an important factor in successfully counselling widows is a great deal of experience in this very specialized helping process.

7

GROUP DISCUSSIONS

The weekly sessions established by the Widows Consultation Center were envisaged as groups of widows who meet together and discuss their feelings, problems, and attempts to establish a more fulfilling set of roles for themselves, under the guidance of trained group discussion leaders. This chapter focuses on the problems and successes of the therapeutic discussion groups as a method for helping widows, concentrating on those details which might be useful in helping a social agency to decide on the advisability of organizing such groups and on some pitfalls to be avoided. It is very possible that in communities which are too small to warrant a specialized center for widows, women's centers or agencies dealing with family problems or problems of the aged could develop such a group program for their widowed clients or members.

There was considerable difficulty in getting this program off the ground. First the Center had to build up enough clients who were interested and who seemed likely to benefit from group discussions. Then a suitable leader had to be found. The first two sessions were held in January 1971, under the leadership of a group therapist from an outside mental health organization. This was, in the words of the Center's director, "a disaster." "She could not control the group, could not deal with their questions." The problem of finding a group leader who will be able to function effectively is one that is likely to occur for other such services. As one of the founders put it, "The fact that someone is a psychiatrist and has a relationship with a well-known institution is not a guarantee that he or she is able to deal with *widows* effectively." It takes very special skills to be able to lead a group of bereaved women in discussions that will be constructive, rather than depressing or upsetting. It is very important to monitor the first couple of sessions closely and to try again with a different leader if the first attempt does not work out.

For a few months, the regular staff members of the Center led the group. However, this was not felt to be fully satisfactory, either. The group began taking one whole day a week away from their time for individual casework. Many group participants wanted to see their social worker individually after the group session. In addition, the group got so large that it obviously needed to be split. At this point, a psychiatric social worker with experience in a bereavement project at a hospital was located and engaged to lead the groups. When she had built up to three groups plus a waiting list, a psychiatrist who herself was a widow was engaged to lead two groups. The groups were segregated on the basis of degree of emotional disturbance, age, and to some extent, socio-economic status, with the widows assigned to the psychiatrist's groups generally those thought by their caseworkers to be "more disturbed." Although the styles and philosophies of these two leaders differed somewhat, both sets of groups seemed to work out well after an initial "shakedown" period.

The main problem with the outside consultants engaged on this basis was the cost ($75 per session paid to the leaders), with many of the widows unable to contribute more than a dollar or two towards this. The Center began exploring and negotiating for arrangements with nearby medical schools and teaching hospitals, to secure the services of psychiatrists in training as group therapy leaders at little or no charge. This sort of arrangement is one which should be explored at the outset by similar social services. During the third year of operation, a male psychiatrist from a nearby hospital began to lead some groups.

THE PURPOSE OF THE GROUPS

When asked "What kinds of things do you see as the goals that you want the women to get out of their participation?" the group leaders saw two main processes: the expression and working through of bereavement (guilt, anger, depression) and the finding of a new identity for themselves. As one leader put it, "My goal for them is *insight* into their problems and insight to see the situation as it really is, so that they can function as things really are, not as they want them to be."

The group leader will help the members to gain insight into their feelings by doing a certain amount of explaining about the psychological mechanisms involved. Our society does not allow the widow to freely express her feelings of guilt and hostility, which are part of the natural reaction to death, and this increases the amount of depression she is likely to experience. As a leader states:

A widespread problem is feeling guilt—"Did I not do all the things I should have done?"—even when the circumstances of the death are not their fault . . . Guilt goes back to many resentments and hostilities which they have repressed because they have not been able to deal with them. Of course, what they say when they come here is "I am so depressed. I am unable to function," and I think I have startled a great many of them when I have said, "Well, of course, depression is basically anger and hostility which hasn't been expressed, which is repressed." This is quite shocking to many of them because it brings them up short.

The problem of finding a new identity is also very emotion-laden, because it involves giving up one's old identity as wife. A leader explains:

One of the main problems of widows has to do with a woman who has been married for so many years losing her husband. There's a whole new adjustment involved in her own identity. She has been a wife for so many years . . . Certain needs are met certain ways. When the person is alone, here she is having invested so much psychic energy into the partner. Here she is with all this hanging in the air . . . No, no, no, I'm still a wife. No, no, no, I'm still nothing. No, no, no, I don't have to find things for myself. No, no. And when the person sees that this "no, no" does not go anywhere, this person is terribly angry.

In addition to these problem areas, bereavement often exacerbates or brings to the surface any other emotional problems that the widow may have had. She is no longer protected by a familiar routine. A leader explains:

I would say that in almost every circumstance these are women who have had difficulties coping long before. The widowhood has thrown it into perspective. They are no longer as protected as they were, or they feel not as protected. What has interested me especially is that as they become more comfortable in the world, they are able to say "I had this same kind of problem before I was married." She had laid it aside, or it hadn't been so prominent. Now, alone, it becomes prominent again. This could be a matter of decision making, or handling friends (men or women) or handling children.

In solving the emotional problems of the group members, the sharing of experiences provided by the group and the immediate feedback from other widows are advantages that the group milieu has over individual counselling, as described by a group leader:

First of all, people who come into the group find out immediately that there are other people in the same situation. There are other people here who have similar feelings, and this alone can be a great factor. You know, after such an experience, people start thinking they are having problems that no one ever had before. This is one function that the group situation can fill. The feeling that they are not unique. Not only are they not unique, but they are *entitled* to have these feelings. They can explore together what appropriate feelings are; what the anger is all about. This is often more effective in making a woman feel she is not crazy than somebody telling her individually that "Everybody feels this way, you are not crazy."

The group is ideally built into a cohesive social unit, with its members having supportive social contacts outside of the formal once-a-week meetings. When one of the members is having a particularly difficult time, the other members keep in touch with her and help her to get through it. The group leaders actively encourage this. For instance [when a particular widow had a problem] "all of the ladies in the group felt concerned about her and called her . . . I have encouraged the women in the group to call her when she wasn't there at a meeting." This not only helps the person that they extend their concern to, but also helps build the cohesiveness of the group, and it helps the person who makes the effort.

SELECTING GROUP PARTICIPANTS

Given the goals of the groups (finding "identity" or "insight" and expressing guilt and anger so that these pent-up feelings do not cause depression, or inability to function), what criteria are used for deciding whether or not a specific widow should join a group?

The recommendation is made by the caseworker and then the case history is reviewed by the prospective group leader to see if the woman will probably fit in one of the groups and benefit from the experience. The first step, recommendation by the caseworker, is somewhat of a hit-or-miss operation. The groups are mentioned in the Center brochure, and some clients ask to join one. When questioned on how they select participants, the caseworkers explained that they tried to decide if the widow would be able to relate to others in the group and find it beneficial. Then they have to be sure that the woman understands what the group is like:

Sometimes they ask to join a group. But they don't always have an understanding of what it means to join a group of other widows who are in a process of working through their bereavement. One of the problems is that you try to explain to them that in order to help themselves they have to relate to the others in the group, and the group process is gradually therapeutic, ideally for everyone in the group. But very often you are not aware of the other members of the group or what has taken place if the other counsellors recommend women for the group. You don't have time to read the records. Consequently, you might have a woman introduced for one time and then she will come back and she will say, "Oh, I couldn't stand that. That was much too depressing. Oh, I heard that one woman talking and talking about her problems." She says, "It wasn't my problem." She only wants to talk about *her* problem. There are a lot of women who want to relate to an individual in a private consultation. Then there are some women who are just anxious to be with other women. They want to chat and talk and socialize and they think that this is what the group is all about.

Overall, 34% of the clients were advised that the groups existed and that they might join one. According to the case records, which are incomplete on this matter, somewhat less than half of these expressed an interest in doing so. At this point, the group leader was given a copy of the case history to review. A group leader explained:

First I read her records and then I see the person and I try to explore with a person how she thinks she would benefit from these sessions. Sometimes they have fantasies about what the group is like, what the therapy is.

Always before going to her first meeting, a woman is contacted by the leader and told what she ought to expect, so that the leader and widow never have to walk into an amorphous situation with a total stranger. The leaders tend to accept most referrals and try to fit them into an existing group if no new group is being formed. However, a leader explains:

I have to think about the person and the group. I rejected one person who was really looking for something else. She was looking for a man. I felt she could not benefit from a group therapy experience. She wanted to be referred to an agency where singles would meet and she would find a man. I saw no point in her joining the group. Another one had sexual problems in the sense that I didn't know how much fantasy and how much reality was there. But with that person I felt something could be worked out in the group. I tried working with the group. She came once. It was good for the group that she was there, but I felt that she needed much more individual help. You have to think about both, the individual and the group.

SIZE, DURATION, AND CHARACTERISTICS OF THE GROUP

The first group grew until about ten people were attending, and this was felt to be too many. Based on her experience with groups of various sizes, one leader said that "Seven is an ideal number. I would say the maximum is definitely not more than nine, allowing for absentees. As for a minimum, you can have three. Even two is fine." The second leader sees from five to eight as the ideal range. As for duration, four months to a year is seen as the optimal length of attendance at weekly sessions. A fairly homogeneous group, in terms of age and socio-economic levels, is felt by the leaders to be preferable. The original split into two groups accomplished this somewhat by accident, with the evening group attracting younger widows who were working during the daytime.

ILLUSTRATIONS OF THE GROUP THERAPY SESSIONS AND PROBLEMS ENCOUNTERED

A good way to understand the way the sessions work and the problems that may arise in working with widows is to look at some excerpts from actual sessions that took place at the Center. These come from the tapes made of each session. The group leaders want to lead the participants toward a *positive* adjustment in their lives, but sometimes the group discussion seems to backfire, at least temporarily, and to make the participants more depressed and less able to cope. It is generally known that such groups can initially have a negative impact on their participants. Here are excerpts from a March 1971 group discussion, shortly after the group began, which illustrate what can happen.

Leader: Welcome again. We meet here every Thursday at 1:30 and we bring into this meeting all of our very sincere feelings and whatever thoughts we have about helping ourselves out of a very trying time. I think today we should talk about—the time comes when our feelings of sadness and guilt do come to some kind of halt. We begin to pull ourselves up, up, to enter the normal stream of things and begin to do the things we *can* do.

Widow 1: I told Mrs. X that since I have been coming here, I think of my husband more than I had. It will be three years in June. I don't feel this is good for me. I was over the loss and in the transition period of what to do about my future.

Leader: Yours was no longer a bereavement problem, but an adjustment problem.

Widow 2: It was three years and ten months for me. I thought I was over it. But I am worse now. When I walked out of here Friday, things that I had suppressed for so long, that I was ashamed to tell my children—I got up today and I broke. I felt I could not go to work. My parents and sister do not know I come here. I'm afraid they'll say I'm crazy.

Widow 3: I feel the same way. It's like a disease. I think the second year, my widowhood is worse.

Widow 4: I met a woman on Sunday; widowed a year and a half. She has still not gotten over it.

Leader: We know how we try our best to pull ourselves together. We are saying that unless you really have worked this out, we will be thrown when things occur. When we get upset, it hasn't been worked out and you are very vulnerable. You must be a whole person again.

Widow 5: I wanted to say that first it is such a shock. You don't really accept it until three years or so, when you realize you're not living.

Widow 2: I kept busy, but now I can't go on.

The session continued on like this for some time.

If these difficult sessions do not depress the participants so much that they drop out, the group can work through the depression and eventually come to support each other. Here is the same group, more or less, one month later. Note that they are generally making supportive comments, rather than comparing miseries.

Widow 1: I felt relieved when I got home last Thursday.
Leader: What you went through is not unique. A lot of people feel fine and suddenly get thrown back into a low state. Do you think this is worth discussing—why it happens?
Widow 2: I felt like taking the pills many a night.
Widow 3: I was tempted too, many a night.
Widow 4: I get strength from the meetings. Each one has something to give. When I'm upset, I can't express myself.
Leader: You're upset now?
Widow 4: I'm trying to get my child in child care. You have to take all these medicals and run around. I'm almost four years a widow. Now I'm ready to get started. The first thing is to get my child taken care of . . .
Leader: You're taking the steps, one at a time.
Widow 4: My children don't help me with anything. I've never learned to be selfish. Now I feel I could do almost anything if I just make my mind up to do it.
Leader: So you're in the first stage of greater self-awareness.
Widow 4: Yes, the awareness comes from knowledge. You have to work for it.
Leader: You have set yourself a goal and are moving toward it. This is terribly important instead of just drifting along.
Widow 5: A short time after my husband was deceased, I said to myself, I have to take care of myself. You can't depend on relatives and friends . . .

Changing the group leader, for whatever reasons, tends to have short-term negative effects. The group feels resentful when its leader is changed, and there is a period of membership instability and heightened aggression against both the new leader and each other for a few weeks. Here are some excerpts from the first session after a new leader was introduced. (This is the same group, three weeks after the supportive session we just looked at.)

Old Leader: Mrs. X will be leading this group from now on. (Makes introductions and leaves.)
New Leader: You must have all kinds of thoughts about having a new leader.
Widow 1: Will we have to start all over again from the beginning?
Leader: You will have to go over some things; I know a little bit about you.
Widow 2: I think we all feel the same way, there is no sense to repeat the same things.
Widow 3: Some things you cannot discuss in a group. It has to be private.
Leader: Why do you think these things cannot be shared?
Widow 4: I feel differently, that is why I come to the group. Certain things I want to get out of my system.
Leader: This is all right. Each one has to be comfortable. My hope is that eventually people will come to the point at which they feel they can share everything.

Widow 4: I don't feel strange with these people. I really found myself. I have learned from these people.

Leader: The only way to find out if you are the only person who has experienced things is to discuss it with others.

Widow 1: We had a gathering—2 said she didn't want to talk to me out of the group. I do talk loud, but nobody's perfect. She said I'm embarrassing her.

Leader: I'm glad you're bringing this up. This is what we are here for.

Widow 2: My husband was five years sick—I got very nervous, but I didn't mean to hurt her.

Widow 1: What she said was very insulting.

Widow 3: I was present at this. 2 did *not* say you embarrassed her.

Widow 2: I'm sorry, I didn't mean it. I didn't say that.

Leader: 2 is apologizing and explaining.

Widow 3: You're very sensitive . . .

Leader: People sometimes say things in a certain way, and it hurts.

Widow: I've noticed I get embarrassed when I'm with this woman. She's so aggressive, says things to strangers.

Leader: So you feel this is the type of reaction we all have in common.

Widow: If you don't like someone, you don't come out and tell them to their face.

Widow 2: If you're going to discuss me like that I'm going to leave [great upset babble of talk] . . .

Widow: What happened to [old leader]?

Leader: Mrs. X. is busy with other things.

Widow: Just one little thing—talk a little bit louder.

Widow: Yes, louder, it is too low.

Leader: Thank you.

Throughout the session, the participants alternately expressed their resentment of the new leader, and fought with each other. Widow 2 went in to see the old leader immediately after this session, in tears, and refused to return to the group in subsequent weeks.

SOME TECHNIQUES USED BY THE LEADERS

The skills and experience that make an effective group leader are obviously impossible to transmit in a brief treatment for a lay audience. We will merely touch on three aspects of the activities of the leader: getting the group started, involving reticent or shy members in the discussions, and controlling the more aggressive members.

A group leader was asked, "When you start a new group, are there any kinds of topics that you feel would be best to introduce first?"

Yes. "Why are we here?" In the beginning, you have to have a certain amount of clarity. You have to know that they are there to work. When I talk I tell them that they are going to *work* . . . At the beginning we talk about life with their husbands and life without their husbands. Before long, the emphasis becomes more and more on their everyday life. But we move back and forth.

When a group has been meeting for awhile, the leaders tend to let the members talk about whatever they want to focus on at that point. A leader commented, "Amazingly, they start right out . . . Some of the ladies have even thought during the week what they want to talk about. Now you asked me what I see as my role. If there is a cohesive and continuing group, then I would see my role as a gradually withdrawing one, so that they take over more and more of the interpretation. I would not want a leadership role, if possible."

In dealing with quiet members, the leaders try to actively draw them into the conversations. One group leader says, "I don't let that happen. I always say, 'Well, Mrs. So-and so, we haven't heard from you this evening. Can you tell us what has been happening, how your work has gone?' Without exception, they respond to that. It calls for intervention."

Overaggressive members also call for the intervention of the leader. The leaders allow a certain amount of the hostilities of the other members to be expressed, and then intervene, saying something like "You should not dominate the group and repeatedly interrupt the others." The leaders can do this without causing the person to drop out of the group once they have established a good relationship with the client:

The main problem is the development of the relationship . . . [based on] evoking feelings and leading the group to assert their feelings out in the open and to support each other . . . [once you have this] you can do all kinds of things because a person knows you are not rejecting her.

PARTICIPANTS' REACTIONS TO THE GROUP DISCUSSION SESSIONS

Follow-up interviews were completed with fifty-five widows who had attended one or more group discussion (or group therapy) sessions through the end of November 1971. Two open-ended questions were used to elicit the opinions of those who reported participating about the usefulness of the sessions: "Tell me about your experiences" and "Do you have any suggestions about how the group discussions might be improved?" Negative reactions centered around two related themes. One is feelings that it was "depressing" or "didn't do any good" for the widows to tell each other about their problems, that they got nothing positive out of this. Among the sixteen comments of this type were the following:

"I had to listen to everyone else's problem. I had my own problem. (Attended three times.)

"I felt overwhelmed listening to them discussing their problems. I didn't get any benefit from it." (Attended once.)

"I found the group discussion to be very depressing. The discussions concerned each woman's tragedy with a rehashing and retelling of the experience. I wanted something more positive. I wanted to look forward to the future; where do I go from here. I didn't want to sit in a mass of self-pity." (Attended twice.)

"They depressed me, more than anything else! They couldn't help me. I just listened." (Attended three times.)

Dr. Robert Weiss tells me that he explicitly discusses this usual reaction with participants during the first meeting of groups for widows. He warns them that they are likely to feel more depressed and upset after the first meeting or two than they have for some time, and explains that this is a normal reaction to openly discussing and thinking about the death and their own widowhood. The Center's policy has been not to raise this spectre. My own judgment is that many fewer widows would have dropped out of the groups after only one or two sessions if the problem had been raised by the group leader.

A second common criticism actually related to a misunderstanding or misuse of the discussion groups. Eleven widows complained because they really wanted the group to serve a social (rather than therapeutic) purpose, and they had not made the friends they were looking for in their group. This included three widows who said that the groups ought to include widowers.

The positive reactions echo the expressed goals of the discussion leaders: the advantages of the group discussion method as a way of gaining a sense of "normality," understanding of oneself, and motivation to go on in new directions.

"I can't talk to relatives and friends, and anything that bothers me I bring it there. I identify with other widows. We have a common grief. I look forward to maybe functioning again." (Attends weekly.)

"I listened to the other people's problems. They felt the way I did. I knew I was normal in my feelings." (Attended twice.)

"They gave me a feeling of strength and acceptance. Seeing them, hearing them, and talking to the other widows was an inspiration and a consolation. It was a relief to know I wasn't alone, the different one. There were others like me, a place for me." (Attended three or four times.)

"It has motivated me and it has helped me . . . I know that it boils down to 'it depends on me.' Whether I would have come to this conclusion without therapy, I don't know, but I like to think it was the group." (Had attended weekly for several months.)

CONCLUSIONS

The group discussion can be a very effective treatment. However, it can also be useless or even detrimental if the woman is not able to relate well enough to the other members and to the leader to allow the interaction to help her understand and work through her problems over a period of time. There are two keys to success. A well-trained discussion leader who is able to deal effectively with the emotional problems of widowhood is crucial, and it may take some trial and error to obtain an effective leader. Secondly, the participants should be chosen carefully. The members of each group should be fairly homogeneous in terms of age and the kinds of problems they have, and they should go into the group with the expectation that it may take several months of participation before they exercise any dramatic changes in their ability to deal with their problems.

Moreover, they should be prepared for the fact that many of them will find themselves temporarily more depressed at the beginning of the group sessions than they have been for some time. Beginning to work through repressed memories and previously unexpressed feelings will be a painful process for many of the participants.

8

SPECIAL SERVICES

In addition to the individual casework services by the social worker and the group therapy sessions, the Widows Consultation Center also developed a set of services which were offered on the basis of referral by the caseworker. A lawyer and a financial consultant were engaged with whom appointments could be made for professional advice. The caseworker could also suggest that a client participate in various social activities, which were arranged by the Center with increasing variety and frequency during the life of the pilot project.

LEGAL CONSULTATION

In New York City the free legal agencies are the Legal Aid Society and the federal agency, Community Action for Legal Services (CALS), and for moderate fees, the legal referral service sponsored by the local bar associations. In most cases the free agencies are not available because of the extremely low income a client must have to be entitled to their services. The referral services turned out to be inadequate in several respects. Many clients already had lawyers but feared that they were not getting adequate advice from them. In other instances it was clear that the lawyers referred from the panel were not really interested in the kind of cases that their clients brought to them, or that they were not able or willing to provide much service for the small fees that the widows could afford to pay.

The Center was fortunate in being able to find a retired lawyer of considerable experience who was willing to give legal service to clients on a volunteer basis. (Although the lawyer does not charge a fee, the Center does ask its usual sliding fee, in order to cover the expenses of arranging the consultation and following up on it by the caseworker.) There was some difficulty in obtaining permission from the Bar Association for this arrangement, as the lawyer explains:

> The professional ethics are that a corporation shall not take a fee and give out legal advice. This outfit takes a $12.50 fee from a widow and I give an opinion. That may or may not be a violation of the ethics; I certainly can't go and represent them in court or draw a document for that fee. Now the Supreme Court of the United States has gone much further than that and held that some unions are allowed to have lawyers that are paid by the union and give advice to the members . . . But our bar association here has not gone that far. I'm not supposed to really give a legal opinion although I have come awfully close to it sometimes. Definitely we cannot do documents such as wills or leases or any other kind of a document, and I cannot go to court, and should not give final advice. If they have a legal problem, I can point it out to them and tell them what they ought to do, and then send them to a lawyer who will do it for them, presumably.

The normal procedure is that if a client has legal problems, the caseworker confers with the lawyer by telephone to find out if he thinks it is a legal problem for which some assistance is possible, to set up an appointment, if it is indicated, and to find out what documents the widow should bring with her. The caseworker then sits in on the legal consultation with the client in most cases. A short written statement of the disposition of the problem and the advice given to the client is given to the widow after the consultation.

In regard to the usefulness or necessity of having the caseworker sit in on the legal consultation, the director of the Center states that the policy is that "if the client is a perfectly clear-thinking woman and it is not a complicated problem, the worker will not sit in. Otherwise, the worker will sit in." As a caseworker explains:

> I find it very helpful for me to sit in while he is talking to her and take notes. Because often they come back to me and say, "Well, Mr. S. said this and this . . ." They are not exactly sure of *what* he said.

If the caseworker has been present for the legal consultation, she can subsequently clarify the situation and the advice for the client.

The lawyer also finds it very helpful to have the social worker present. He says:

> They seem to have a kind of control over these widows that I don't get. They have talked with these widows and have a certain amount of confidence from the widow, and it helps to steady the whole thing . . . If the widow gets running a little wild, they bring them around to the point. Also, they say if the widow seems to be shocked or hesitant, "Well, Mr. S. is an

experienced lawyer and he knows what he is talking about; you had better listen to him." This straightens them out right away.

The Center volunteer lawyer finds that the emotional upset accompanying widowhood is one reason why the clients seem to need what they consider an impartial source of advice—that is, one which cannot possibly reap financial gain from the advice being given. He explains:

I think most of the people who come in here are just a little bit unstable mentally. They don't know enough to take the word of an attorney. They get frightened about whether they should pay the fees. In some cases, they are right about kicking about the fees. But mostly, they are just a little bit unstable and they're running around asking a lot of people questions. I bet they've been other places than here making inquiries. They are hard to pin down when you talk to them. It takes a long time to get them to the point. They are talking all over the place about their sufferings, and a lot of stuff that has nothing to do with the legal points involved. I sit patiently by and listen to it. Now the lawyers they go to may be annoyed with this, and this may make them a little brusque with the widow, and that frightens them. They don't have the patience to listen to these stories that have nothing to do with the legal problem . . .

I think it's very helpful to these widows, who are very often afraid of the lawyers they go to, and think they're demanding too much. To come to somebody who is impartial, you might say, and who can point out the problem to them and say, "Well, this lawyer was right in what he wanted to do or he was wrong or he took too much money from you." That's the type of thing that is apparently very reassuring to them, and is what I'm doing, mostly.

At the time the lawyer was interviewed, he had handled only about fifteen cases. Almost all of these had to do with problems of settling the estate. Most of the questions have to do with taxes that must be paid, probating the will, and so forth. The lawyer says:

In the settlement of the estates of their husbands, they fairly often come quite early after the death. They've been to a lawyer and they want to know if he's doing the right thing, and whether he's taking the right amount of money. Many of them have been gouged right from the start and my feeling is that a lawyer who takes on an estate should not take a retainer fee. He should specify that his fee will be a percentage of the estate when he gets through. Now some of these fellows are grabbing money from the widows right off the bat, and doing very little for them . . .

The widows are scared of their lawyers lots of times. Usually these lawyers have been attorneys for the husband during his life, or some friend has recommended them, but they don't turn out to be good in handling estates . . .

They're mostly frightened, frightened of the lawyer they've been talking to, because they think he's bossing them around, and they feel that they have to give in to him on very point and let him run them, and they don't like that. And I have to tell them they're the boss, that they're the ones who say what they're going to do, whether they'll follow his advice or not. That's one point that I make with them.

In handling the widow's problem, the lawyer states:

With first things first, ask them whether the will has been probated, and somebody's been appointed executor, or if there is no will, whether there is an administrator. And then the next question is, what's been done about the estate taxes, because they come up very soon. In New York State, for instance, you have to make a temporary payment within six months. If you don't, and if you don't pay at least 80% of the final tax, you run into penalties. Under the federal estate tax, which goes in for estates over $60,000, you have to pay the tax and file the return within nine months, so that all comes up very fast. Usually the next questions are what property is there that's in joint names and a lot of them have joint property with their husbands. And they can't understand why they can't draw the money from the bank. And I have to point out to them that those joint accounts are taxable, that certainly in New York State the banks, unless the account is less than $2,000, will not let it be drawn out without what we call a waiver issued by the tax commission, which they will do after they've gotten a record of what the bank account is so they know how to follow it up in the future. They can't understand why they can't get that money. Then they have problems with transferring stock in a joint name; they run into waivers, and they run into affidavits of residence and all sorts of things, here and there. I tell them either their lawyer ought to handle it, or to go to their broker, and let him run them through. Because there are various kinds of restrictions on those transfers according to what states the company is organized in and those are the questions that come through, mostly.

Whether the case has to do with the estate, or more rarely, with suits for death or problems with Social Security or some other type of legal question, the lawyer functions to "pinpoint the problem and tell the widow what's what and what they can do about it and what they can expect from the lawyer that they have hired or intend to hire."

Because of the ethical restrictions referred to above, where legal action or drawing of documents is involved or research cases and precedents required, it is still necessary to refer the client to an outside lawyer. For this purpose, the Center has selected a panel of attorneys who have agreed to charge moderate fees commensurate with the means of the widows sent to them by the Center. When referrals to outside attorneys are made, the Center is always careful to provide several names and to leave the final choice to the widow herself, in order to avoid both legal liability or the appearance of being in league with a particular lawyer.

There are no data available for evaluating the helpfulness or effectiveness of this legal consultation process, since it was begun after the cut-off date for the follow-up interviews with clients. The same evaluation problem occurs for the financial consultation service, to be described below, which had only one or two of its clients included in the follow-up. The members of the staff, however, give an enthusiastic high rating based on feedback from their clients, who seem to feel grateful and pleased about the quality of the advice they receive. Given the fact that there are no other services for a widow to approach with confidence if she suspects that she is being over-charged or that she may be getting poor legal advice, it is highly recommended to other services that they too attempt to find a retired attorney to provide legal service.

FINANCIAL CONSULTATION

Providing advice on money management for the minority of widows with enough assets to worry about turned out to be a thornier subject than was originally anticipated. If a widow is sure that she wants to talk to a stockbroker or a banker or even to an insurance agent, there is no problem. The Center maintains lists of representatives from well-established firms from which the client can choose. The Center bends over backwards not to recommend one specific organization in any case. But if the widow's problem was one of deciding how to allocate her money, there is no existing source of expert advice to which she could be referred that was obviously unbiased. The Center staff certainly did not feel competent to give this kind of advice.

The solution reached by the Center was to arrange for a nationally known author and lecturer on personal investment to be attached to the Center as a financial advisor. Whenever at least five clients have said that they would like to confer with him, he comes to the Center for a day of appointments. The arrangement works very satisfactorily, except for the administrative problem of spending time on the telephone to find a day when everyone can make it. A caseworker says:

It's of tremendous value to have Mr. X. so involved. He really is interested in our clients . . . He is always willing to set up a day and talk to these wom-en . . . The clients have reported that he was very sound, conservative, and interested in their particular situation. He tried to understand something of their life style and where they are in their planning for their future and so forth.

The financial consultant is given a preliminary form filled out by the applicant outlining her assets, liabilities, her requirements, and other data. Having reviewed the widow's assets and needs, he explains in practical terms the options open to the client. With the information given to her, she makes her own decisions with regard to investments, brokers, etc. The advice from the consultant, for instance, might take the form of advising the client to put a certain proportion in a savings account and the rest in common stock in, say, oils or chemicals. It does not take the form of a specific instruction like "buy twenty-five shares of IBM" or "open an account at First National City Bank for $5,000."

The financial service is described in the Center's brochure, so that most of the clients to whom it is suggested are those who specifically ask about it. In addition, the caseworker may suggest it

when they seem to need this kind of thing; if you see they are squandering ... Sometimes they think they have a huge sum of money, and you know that it's not huge enough for anyone to get along on over a long-term pull. Then, I say that they may be interested in seeing Mr. X. Then you have the one who is holding back on everything because she thinks that she will never be able to live through her life without going on assistance, and you know that her finances are well established. Then sometimes reassurance by a financial advisor is very helpful ... However, if she has someone whom she is seeing through her other resources, fine. I don't want it to appear that we are touting anything. We are not trying to build up any business through this, but rather offering a service which she can accept or not accept.

In describing the financial problems brought to him by the widows and the advice he gives, the financial consultant notes:

In 90% of the cases, the question is how to make the best use of the money on hand. If a woman is elderly—sixty-five plus—I generally prescribe high grade bonds, which today yield from 7½ to 7¾ percent. While these do not offer much protection against inflation, the generous income (over what may be expected from most stocks) is enough—I feel—to cushion the effects of inflation for about ten years or more.

If a woman is in her fifties or so, she must have part of her money in common stocks in the hope that market appreciation plus dividend increase will help her offset inflation over the next fifteen or twenty years.

There are two kinds of problems that are encountered again and again. One is that financially unsophisticated widows do not understand that the real cost of owning a home is much more than the out-of-pocket costs, and this must be explained in some detail. The financial consultant provided an illustration.

The classic example would be a widow with only modest capital continuing to live in a $65,000 home because "it is all paid for." A $65,000 house, I have to show her, costs at least $6,500 "rent" a year—whether she owns it down to the ground or not—since $65,000 today can earn close to $5,000 a year if invested in high grade bonds, and taxes, heat, repairs, etc., easily add $1,500 more. This example always proves a shocker to a woman who thinks she has her "rent" assured by continuing to live in a big house.

A second kind of unwise financial thinking frequently encountered is the widow's basing investment and spending on what she thinks her husband would have wanted, or what she thinks would be good for her children, rather than in terms of her own best interests. Often, notes the consultant,

I must prove to them that the stocks their husbands bought are not suited to their needs as a widow. This sometimes causes a sentimental upset since many feel they are being disloyal to their husband's memory. Many cannot bring themselves to sell out at a loss speculative stock which has been held for years, not realizing that the loss is already there, whether they sell or not, and that meanwhile, they have X thousands of dollars producing no income.

Another problem: putting concern for children—often financially successful—ahead of the widow's immediate needs. It takes a bit of talking to get these widows to look after No. 1. For example, many insist on maintaining expensive insurance policies although there is no need for this protection.

A problem for many widows is that they do not have any idea how to use their capital in order to be able to feel assured that it will not all be spent long before they die. As the consultant points out, there is no sure solution to this problem, but he has a standard kind of advice:

I cannot tell a sixty-year-old woman with, say $50,000 capital, that she can spend $3,000 or $5,000 a year from capital and not have to worry about running out of money before she runs out of breath . . . There is no way a mortal can decide how much capital one should spend a year since there is no way of knowing how long she will live. If the woman is around sixty-five to seventy or older, a lifetime annuity will guarantee her a generous income for the rest of her life. If she is younger, annuity rates are not good enough. In that case, I suggest bonds for five or ten years, and then a shift to an annuity.

One problem that the financial consultant encountered was that sometimes when he advised widows to buy bonds, they ended up being pressured by brokers into buying mutual funds, because the commissions are much higher on mutual funds than on bonds. Also, he notes:

In a few cases, the women were so elderly and unsophisticated that I feared my suggestions would never be carried out, or even understood . . . I suppose it would be helpful if the Center could follow through on my suggestions, although this would involve more staff.

A possibility here would be for the Center staff to sit in on the financial consultations for clients who seem easily confused, just as they do for the legal consultations. The problem here is that many widows are extremely reluctant to reveal full details of their financial situation to the caseworker, and the very person who might need further explanation and prodding from the caseworker to carry out the financial advice is also likely to be the most suspicious and distrustful of intervention in financial matters. Besides being time-consuming, in other words, taking on such a role might interfere with the therapeutic relationship between caseworker and client.

SOCIAL AND RECREATIONAL ACTIVITIES

The individual client who expresses a need for new friends or activities may be invited to participate in one or more of the activities sponsored by the Center for this purpose: a monthly tea, monthly discussion workshops or seminars, trips, a Sunday afternoon social group meeting at the local YWHA, or a small widow-to-widow program.

Monthly teas are usually held for widows from a specific section of the metropolitan area. According to the director of the Center:

Groups of women thought to be compatible by reason of background, locality, or other factors are invited to meet, in the hopes that they may get to know each other and form friendly associations. The expectation is that this will make it easier for them to pursue together recreational, educational, or other interests.

Along the same lines, outings or trips have been arranged by the Center, including theatre parties, weekend bus trips, and tours of local points of interest.

The seminars or workshops are organized around specific topics and usually include an outside speaker. During the spring of 1972, for instance, the topics included "On Your Own," "Recovery from Bereavement," "Vocational Problems and Opportunities in a Fast Changing World," a "Consciousness Raising" session, and a discussion of a book, *Loneliness.*

These events were one-time only affairs and were generally held during the week when Center staff members could lead the meetings. A need was felt for more ongoing social activities for some clients, especially to fill their weekends. During the third year of the Center's operation a part-time worker was engaged to organize a regular Sunday afternoon social group, which was held at a nearby YWHA, as well as the other social activities.

For this weekend group, as well as for the more formal meetings, the social workers submit weekly lists of clients of theirs who they think should be invited. Twenty to forty women is the usual number attending. At the Sunday social group, the worker is there, and she provides the coffee and cookies, but only a minimal kind of leadership. The Center's director describes the Sunday socials as follows:

The worker talks to them but she doesn't actually do much talking. She lets the women talk among themselves. It's mainly a social get-together where people get to know each other. Let me give you excerpts from a sample report which I think is the best way to gauge what goes on there. . .

What happened [at this particular meeting] was she took a few minutes to tell them exactly how many women were there; there were thirty-nine that day. She took a few minutes to tell the new people what it was all about; there were twelve that day. It was interesting to note that when Mrs. X. expressed a wish to meet other clients who were living in Forest Hills, immediately two other women gave their names and responded. Arrangements were made for them to meet outside the group. Then two black clients explained why they hadn't been there before and their pleasure in being there . . . Then another new client announced that on Saturday there was the Manhattan Women's Political Caucus and a lot of women said they would go. Then somebody else asked for volunteers in connection with getting out a mailing for the December 12 benefit for the Brooklyn Academy . . .

A dozen women volunteered to go and they did go on Sunday, and they helped with the mailing. And then another woman invited all of those who were there that day to come next week to her home to see films and have a social afternoon. About twenty women were interested and were going . . .

I won't go into all the details, but the women were cooperative with each other in listening with interested sympathy . . . There is a growing cohesiveness in the group.

In a report to the Center's board, the director said:

From our brief experience we have learned that social activities such as mentioned above are highly desirable and may fill one of the greatest needs of our clients. We are accordingly addressing ourselves to developing further this aspect of our program, hoping eventually to integrate our clients into existing community recreational and educational facilities. To attain this objective requires our working with the client until she is able to take advantage of a community facility, and working with the facility to help them understand the transitional role that is required.

A social worker expanded on this idea. She said:

We see these women as coming together socially for a certain period of time and then moving on, to either their own little clique, in the group that they formed within the social activity, or finding their own way.

The addition of the part-time worker in charge of social activities facilitated a much-expanded program in this area, which was not available to the widows included in the follow-up survey. The social activities director reported in the fall of 1972, after about six months of work, that:

Bringing the women together at the "Y" indicated a forward movement in the direction of community involvement. They were able to identify with other than their own homes, or with the Center, as a safe and cozy place to come to. To effectuate still further fanning out into the community and enriching their regimen with the cultural life of the theatre, music and the dance, a program was initiated to provide our women with tickets for the various cultural events in the community.

Personnel from the Lincoln Center Complex, the Metropolitan Opera, City Center, Public Theatre, and the Brooklyn Academy of Music responded with the utmost generosity and interest on behalf of the women.

For instance, the American Ballet Theatre donated a total of seven hundred tickets during their six-week season, and Philharmonic Hall gave about three hundred for their Mostly Mozart Festival.

WIDOW-TO-WIDOW

A fledgling widow-to-widow program was organized by one caseworker in order to encourage very lonely and troubled clients to keep in touch with one another and the Center. A client of hers, acting as a volunteer, served as the focus of a telephone communications network. The worker kept her supplied with a list of ten or twelve other widows, either from her own current cases or those of other workers, whom the volunteer called regularly. The volunteer came into the Center one day a week to do this. The worker who organized it said:

She's very good with them, and they love to hear from one widow to another. She is able to give them the feeling that they are being cared for, that we are interested in how they are getting along . . . She also visits the ladies if they need her to visit. She takes it on herself to take long trips on her own expense. In addition, the volunteer widow serves to alert the caseworker if any of the widows she talks to seems to be in need of help.

One reason why this aspect of the Center's program has not been expanded is lack of space for the telephoning. It is felt that this should be done from the Center. The organizing caseworker says:

The thing is that this should not be done just by the widow herself from her own home. There is something very supportive and authentic in her doing it right from the office. It gives her the feeling of being part of the service that is being given.

The New York Widows Consultation Center had many reservations about expanding their widow-to-widow program, however. As one caseworker put it:

I feel that such a program would have to be supervised extremely carefully. I don't think that by virtue of being a widow one necessarily knows the right things to say or do. Therefore, I would have to be very sure that the person whom I would utilize in this fashion knew where to tread and where not to. In my own patient load, I find that many of them are so troubled themselves that they are not at the point where they could give . . . I'm not sure that I think this is the best form of therapy.

In a smaller community, where the widows could visit face-to-face without travelling long distances to strange neighborhoods, this type of social network as an adjunct to the professional social workers would probably be more feasible. In the Canadian Centre in Winnipeg, for example, the widow-to-widow program involves three aides reporting to the professional director, who also does all of the individual casework. Each of the three visiting widows works about fifteen hours a week. These are women who have been widowed a minimum of three years and have been chosen because of their sensitivity and their appropriateness as role models. The goals of the program are described as follows:

1. To offer a role model—a widow who has made it, who has lived through a smiliar experience, survived and coped.
2. To offer supportive experience to the widow—literature and experience stress the importance of verbalizing, as a means of coming to grips with the death of the husband, and the Visiting Widow functions as a mechanism to enable the widow to verbalize and to be a safe individual to verbalize to.
3. To offer hope to the widow at a time of despair—to let them know someone cares, society cares, to rationalize and accept their grief work as normal.
4. To offer some information on being a widow, for there are no other similar learning experiences in life, and to offer resources to assist the widow in the process of reestablishing herself.
5. To offer information about the resources available to widows in the community—notably in the Centre. (DeGraves, 1975).

The Canadian director explains:

The model chosen is that of aggressive outreach to the newly created widow, on the basis that literature, experience, and the statements of widows confirm that a recent widow would not be likely to reach out to the centre for assistance, even though such assistance is meaningful and necessary.

This outreach policy received strong support in a follow-up survey of widows contacted by the program, 91% of whom reported that they would not have been likely to contact the Winnipeg Centre on their own.

During the twelve-week pilot period for this program (April to June 1975), the Canadian Centre's widow-to-widow program operated as follows:

Names of widows whose husbands were under sixty-five years of age at death are taken from newspaper obituaries. At eight weeks following the death the widow is assigned to a Visiting Widow (VW), assignment being made on the basis of proximity to the home of the VW and similarity in national or religious background. The VW sends a letter to the widow setting an appointment time and giving a number for the widow to telephone if she wishes to change or cancel the appointment. If she does not hear from the widow, the VW calls at her home at the appointed time. The VW then relies on her own assessment of the widow's needs in determining what help is required and whether to continue visits.

During the first three months of this program, 118 widows were contacted. Fifty-one percent of this sample accepted service (this proportion has risen in subsequent months, possibly because newspaper publicity concerning the service has made it more acceptable to the new widow), 33% refused service, and 16% could not be located . . .

Some minor changes have been made in response to client feedback during the trial period: (1) the interval between husband's death and initial contact was changed from 6 weeks to 8 weeks, (2) the letter to the widow was changed to avoid the impression of assuming the widow had problems, (3) in visiting widows in outlying suburbs the VW's have made it a practice to telephone to confirm the appointment before making a long trip to the home (DeGraves, 1975).

Data on the relative costs of such a program, as compared to the New York Center's service model emphasizing individual counselling by a professional social worker, will be given in the final chapter.

9

THE EFFECTIVENESS OF THE CENTER

Widows were traditionally an object of charity in Western nations, but in recent years they have become a relatively neglected group, as ethnic minorities have become the focus of most government efforts to deal with poverty. On the institutional level, one can report a subjective evaluation that the Center has been effective in calling attention to the problems of widows and in stimulating new or existing social welfare services to reach out to help them. A steady stream of inquiries from communities around the United States and abroad asking about what can be done to start a service similar to the Center attests to this impact.

The director of the offshoot Canadian Centre also finds that there is a great need for such a public education and information function, which she accomplished through media interviews and through speaking to women's groups. In this way, the public in both nations has become more aware of the emotional and social problems of widowhood, the ways in which one may prepare for widowhood, and the ways in which family and friends may be helpful.

As for the effectiveness of the Center for the particular widows who have come through its doors, we have some sources of data, but none of these is a totally satisfactory measure of its impact on the lives of its clients. First of all, we must decide what we mean by effectiveness. One cannot expect that a few hours of counselling by a social worker can solve problems that are often so complex, and so embedded in the sexism and agism of society itself. If it can help the widow to understand and accept her situation, and to begin to take steps to build a more satisfying life, then it has succeeded.

The main criteria of effectiveness used in this study are the widows' own feelings about whether or not the Center had helped them, obtained during the follow-up interviews. In each problem area that a widow reported having at the time she came to the Center, she was asked if the Center tried to help in any way, and if so, whether this attempt had actually improved the situation. There were also some questions which asked for overall assessments of the effectiveness of the Center, and for what the Center had done which had been most helpful. In this chapter we will first look at the assessments of the Center's effectiveness in helping with specific types of problems. Then we will turn to the overall effectiveness of the Center and how this varies by number of visits by the client and with various characteristics of the widows. A few case histories will be presented to illustrate more concretely than do the statistics the kinds of case histories associated with the greatest and least client satisfaction with the Center. Finally, we will look in detail at the costs of the services provided by the Widows Consultation Center and at alternative service models which are not as expensive and which could more easily be adopted in other communities.

Help with emotional areas stands out as the type of problem with which widows felt the Center had been most helpful. Overall, 53% of all widows who were questioned about this area said that the Center had been helpful to them. This is followed by help with financial matters (16% of those answering questions on this problem area reported they had been helped) and family problems (15%). In other problem areas, only a small proportion of clients felt that they had really been helped: 9% in dealing with government agencies; 9% in finding new friends or activities; 6% with finding a job; 5% with finding living quarters, and only 2% with problems of missing male companionship. (It should be noted that the 9% helped with finding new friends or activities refers to a client group which did not have the opportunity to attend the regular Sunday social meeting, which began later.)

These evaluations by clients correspond to those of the staff, which felt that they were most effective in individual counselling on emotional problems, and least effective in trying to help widows cope with the shortage of suitable jobs and apartments in the metropolitan area.

EFFECTIVENESS IN HELPING WITH EMOTIONAL PROBLEMS

We noted above that 53% of the widows questioned about emotional problems during the follow-up interview said that the Center had helped them in this area. (Only widows who had been widowed five years or less were asked about "becoming emotionally adjusted to their widowhood." It would have been better to ask all clients questions about emotional problems related to bereavement, rather than assuming that long-term widows had already made their adjustments, good or bad.) But 21% reported that they did not have any emotional problems at the time they came to the Center. Fourteen percent said that their caseworker or someone else at the Center had tried to help them with emotional problems, but that they had not actually improved the situation. Twelve percent said that they had emotional problems, but they did not feel that anyone at the Center had tried to help solve them. This breaks down into half (6%) who explained that they did not mention emotional problems or ask for any help in this area, and half who gave some other explanation or no reason why the Center did not try to help. Putting these figures together and looking only at those widows who *had* emotional problems at the time they came to the Center and who mentioned them, a very impressive 73% of such clients reported that the Center had helped improve their emotional problems.

The staff concurs with this assessment, as illustrated by the following excerpt from an interview with a caseworker during October 1972:

Evaluator: Overall, in what areas would you say that you have been most helpful to the clients who come here? What is the biggest need that widows have that the Center does meet at this time?
Caseworker: I think that the greatest need that widows have is their feeling of loneliness and isolation. Even in a populated community with family around, they feel very isolated, because everybody does carry his pain alone. But if you feel that you have someone to help you carry it, then perhaps tomorrow might be better. There are concrete things that we can do, too, and we certainly do. But if I were to say what we do the very best, it is the kind of emotional help that they cannot receive any place else, because nobody else, unless they have gone through the numbers that we have so that they can see a pattern, is capable of doing that . . . They know that we understand.

Since both clients and staff feel that emotional problems, especially those connected with bereavement, are the area in which the Center has been most effective, let us look at this area in more detail.

To the question, "Overall, what was the most helpful thing that the Widows Consultation Center did for you, if anything?" the answers of the clients reflect the efforts of the caseworkers and group discussion leaders to deal with loneliness, grief, and other emotional problems associated with widowhood: 37% of all clients reported that listening and giving sympathy had been the one thing that helped them most. Here is how some of the clients described the emotional support they received:

"Sometimes the right word by the right person can make all the difference. When I walked out I felt wonderful, like I had something to go back to."

"Their value is in sitting and listening sympathetically to your problem, and then it's not a problem anymore . . . They will just let you talk it all out."

"They made me feel like I was a person and that I was important."

"Most of all, they made me feel like a human being."

"It made me feel good to have someone to talk my heart out to."

"You don't have to hide anything. You could speak freely. Mrs. X was wonderful, so appealing. She gives you hope that you're not lost. When I left the place, I had a good feeling that there are good people in the world."

"I can say they helped—I can't say how—maybe by welcoming me and listening with respect to what others would consider feeling sorry for yourself."

There are occasional testimonies of a "minor miracle." For instance, here are excerpts from one follow-up interview:

I didn't think I could be helped, and I walked in with a chip on my shoulder. Mrs. X was the loveliest person I ever met. When I walked out, I was a different person. She changed my whole life . . . I had known my husband was dying for four years, and I had lived a life of subterfuge. I felt terribly guilty and blamed myself for his death. I would see my husband all over the house. I couldn't sleep, because I thought that if I went to sleep, I would die. I couldn't handle any of this. She talked all of this out with me and convinced me that it was not my fault and that I felt his presence because I loved him so much. When I walked out, I was so healed. I was a completely different person.

OTHER PROBLEM AREAS

Table 9.1 summarized the clients' reports on the nature of the Center's efforts in problem areas other than emotional adjustment. It enables us to sort out those areas in which the Center did not help many of its clients because no such problems existed in the first place from those in which the efforts were fruitless.

Let us begin with the area that stands out as being the one with which the Center was helpful to practically no one at all—dealing with problems of missing male companionship. (The question asked included problems of sexual frustration, but no women admitted this as a problem area. The questions on male companionship were not included in the telephone interviews, so that the data are based only on 114 personal interviews.) Almost a quarter of the clients questioned said that this had been a problem for them when they came to the Center, but no one there tried to help them deal with it.

The caseworkers admit that this is a "sensitive area" and that they never bring this up themselves and also hesitate to try to give advice when a woman raises it herself. It is an area fraught with fears on the part of the clients, as pointed out previously in the discussion of problem areas. One sensed during the follow-up interviews that many widows who quickly claimed that male companionship or sexual fulfillment were "not a problem" for them "did protest too much." Here are some comments made during follow-up interviews which further illustrate how unable many of the women are to face this problem:

[From a woman who said "not a problem"] "I miss my husband, that's true. If I met someone I like . . . But just to pick someone up, I'd rather die first . . . Everyone I know is married. I have no opportunities."

"I don't think about it. If you don't play with fire, you won't get burned."

"I'm looking for companionship, but I don't know if I'm looking for *male* companionship. I'm frightened to even want to look for it because I don't know if I could face it if they propositioned me."

Table 9.1

Clients' Evaluation of Center's Helpfulness in Various Problem Areas

Problem Area	% helped among those telling Center of problem	% of total clients Center helped	Center tried, did not help	Did not try, client did not mention problem	Did not try, other explanation	No problem	Total
Family relationships	51	15	9	8	5	63	100
Finding a job	14	6	26	3	6	58	100
Living quarters	22	5	7	9	8	71	100
Finding new friends or activities	24	9	17	11	13	49	100
Dealing with Social Security or other agencies	60	9	5	4	0	82	100
Male companionship	9	2	3	8	15	71	99
Managing money or making ends meet	33	16	11	8	23	42	100

Source: Follow-up interviews.

Here are some of the comments of caseworkers on this subject:

"If you have a woman who is widowed for two–four months, unless she initiates this discussion, it is almost a slap to some of them to even mention it. They are so involved in their loss. The very thought of even going out . . . Perhaps at your follow-up a year later, they don't remember that at the time they came here, they were not ready. They weren't even ready to meet another woman, no less a man."

"Perhaps there are things that we could do, but there are always hazards in trying to involve men and women under the auspices of an agency. I guess what you could do is involve them in seminars, things that are relatively innocuous and "academic." I will make a connection between one woman and another, but I would never do this for a man and a woman."

"As for wishes to remarry or find male companions—we tell them we are not set up to give help with this directly. We can make some suggestions about what kinds of activities to join where they might meet men."

In this area then, the Center is not helpful because they specifically do not wish to serve as a dating agency or source of "advice to the lovelorn."

Jobs and housing are also areas with which the Center has not been helpful to many, but for quite different reasons. Here, the Center would like to be of help, but the reality of the situation in the metropolitan area makes it difficult to accomplish very much. This is especially evident in the area of finding jobs; we saw in Table 9.1 that 26% of the clients report that the Center tried to be of help but failed. Here is an exchange with one of the caseworkers which highlights the frustrations encountered:

Evaluator: What procedures do you use if a woman comes in and says, "I need a job. I can't live on the little bit of money I have."
Caseworker: Your heart drops. If she's seventy-two years old and she's not attractive and has no education and no skill, but she doesn't want to babysit and she doesn't want to work any place but between this block and that block, then your heart drops. You try to motivate her to accept certain work within her ability at this time, saying that perhaps as she gets her feet wet in something like volunteer work or something not quite to her liking, perhaps from there she can move to something else, or perhaps she will be happy where she is. But this is a tremendous frustration. With some, I am very honest in saying that I know that the job market is very difficult, and we must realistically look at what you can do.
Evaluator: So that realistically you see your main function as to motivate them to take something less than they thought they could get?
Caseworker: Even those lesser things are often difficult. Sometimes you just have to be very frank and say, "As much as I would like to help you with this problem, this is the way the situation is."

Another reason why so many of the clients feel that the Center has not helped them with their job problems is that at least some of the personnel assume a request for help in finding a job is not the "real, underlying" problem that a widow has, but rather often a "handle" for getting help with emotional problems. Here is how one caseworker explained it:

Caseworker: Actually, if they come to us for employment, we understand that they are having a problem other than employment. The job market is so bad that people who come with any emotional or physical shortcomings are usually screened out of any possibility. We do give them help when they ask for it because we want them to feel that we are responding to their need, and if it's possible to get it for them, it is a very cheering fact. Work is therapeutic in itself. It sustains a person's sense of value in the community.
Evaluator: If you were able to start any kind of experiment to help more widows to find a job, is there anything you can think of that might be helpful?
Caseworker: Like, opportunities to gain a marketable skill? In order to gain a skill, the person has to be able and willing to concentrate on the learning process. And the widows who come here, for the most part, are not yet pulled together. They are fragmented by grief and they do not know in which direction to turn first. They catch at whatever they are told: "Get a job," "go out, don't stay in the house"—they are told many things and when they come here they select one or several of these things and ask us to help them because they can't yet find the strength for these things. We don't push them in all directions. We say, "Yes, we have these opportunities when you are ready." But if all you do is push her into it, you have offered her very little except again the feeling of being confronted and inability to move on. So what you have to do is first help the person to regain a sense of integration of the self. So that a course of training has to be geared to a woman's readiness to move into it. When she is ready, she no longer has to seek us to do it. There are ways in the community. We do give her these little helping facts. You can go here and there, but we have discovered that they don't really take hold immediately. First, they need to get hold of the self again and make it a working, productive self.

The result of such assumptions and the lack of jobs for older women without experience has been frustration and disappointment on the part of many clients. Here are some of the comments they made during the follow-up interviews:

"They sent me on a job, but I didn't want that kind of a job . . . When they sent me for a job, they should have followed through. They should have called to see if I was working or to try to get me another job."
"They sent me to an agency, but they had nothing for me."
"They wrote a few letters and tried to give me some leads . . . None of them ever led to anything . . . It would be nice if they could be more of an employment agency and have a file of jobs."
"They were nice and made two appointments for me. But they did not work out."
(From a woman who said that finding a job was a very "serious" problem) "I got $92 a month from Social Security. It wasn't enough. If I didn't find a job, I'd have to go on relief and I was scared . . . They sent me to an office, but it needed filing and I'm not experienced. I suppose I could have gone back and they would have tried some more."

"They sent me to Mature Temps but that was not for me. I was forty-nine. The people there were much older . . . They should send you to better places. I was disappointed. They could do nothing for me."

"I had no husband and no job and needed work. She had me fill out an application. Told me she had no work for me, to call her. I called twice but she had nothing."

At the very least, it would appear that the Center should follow through on more of the job referrals it makes, giving additional encouragement and suggestions when the initial suggestions are not fruitful. Since almost half of the widows who come to the Center have a problem in finding a job, the Center's ineffectiveness in this area cannot be dismissed lightly.

Housing is an area with which the staff has felt almost totally powerless to deal, as illustrated by the following comments by caseworkers in October 1972:

Caseworker: I've gotten to the point where I say that I am sorry, but I will be unable to help you with this. I know that I can tell them to make applications here and there. But generally when they come, they can't wait for some housing authority application to be processed, for umpteen months and years. Even for physical problems for which a doctor has said that the person must get out of her apartment or neighborhood, you very, very rarely move any agency into action. There are long lists, and people don't move.
Interviewer: What about the area of the widows who are unhappy about their living quarters?
Caseworker: The reality is that there is very little that we can do for her. If a woman is hard pressed financially, you can direct her to the central office where they have women from the housing division trying to help with problems. Otherwise, there is very little that we can offer except for the middle income housing applications. We follow up with letters to the housing authorities, and I've had a few successes. But not enough.

Having examined the areas in which the Center has largely failed to help its clients, let us turn to some other problems with which there has been somewhat more success.

MONEY MANAGEMENT

The problems which were included in this area are extremely varied, from needing a few more dollars a month at the poverty level to struggling with large estates at the upper end of the socio-economic spectrum. Most widows (58%) said that they had some sort of problem in this area when they came to the Center, but slightly over half of these felt that the Center did not try to help. This was especially true for the less educated clients. Sixty-two percent of widows with less than a high school education who had money management problems felt that the Center had not tried to help solve them, compared with 30% of women with some college education. On the other hand, it was the most highly educated women who were most likely to report that the Center had been helpful in this area. The other measures of socio-economic status used in this study (husband's occupation, race, present total household income) show the same thing: the better off the widow, the more likely she was to report that the Center had helped with financial problems. This is in line with the kinds of facilities the Center had and its policies. It really cannot do much to deal with poverty, since it has no funds to dispense. Its legal and financial consultants, on the other hand, are most likely to be of assistance to widows with fairly substantial assets.

FINDING NEW FRIENDS AND ACTIVITIES

Fifty-one percent of clients reported that finding new friends or leisure activities was a problem for them when they came to the Center, but less than two fifths of these women felt the Center had helped them with this. The social activities and "seminars" would seem on the face of it to be the main mechanism for introducing clients to other women who want to make friends, and there is a statistical relationship between having this as a problem area and having been invited to social activities connected with the Center. However, 70% of the women for whom this was a serious problem had not attended any social activities sponsored by the Center. There is also a definite relationship between the number of social activities attended and the feeling that the Center had helped in finding new friends or activities, with 29% of those attending two or more social activities reporting that the Center had helped them in finding new friends, compared to 5% among those attending no such activities. On the other hand, a large proportion of the women attending social gatherings did not feel that they had a problem in finding new friends to begin with; many others did not perceive these events as having been an attempt to create a situation in which they could meet friends; and many widows who reported finding new friends and activities to be a problem had not been invited to any of the Center events.

In summary, it would seem that there should have been a better matching of needs to invitations and a more direct emphasis on stimulating further social contacts among those attending. The regular Sunday gatherings at the "Y" had not started at the time the follow-up interviews were conducted, however, so that these shortcomings probably would have been somewhat alleviated by that program.

The reactions of those who did attend social activities tended to be favorable: thirty-seven of the forty-nine women who talked about the social gatherings during the follow-up interview made positive comments, four had mixed reactions, and eight made negative comments. Typical of the positive remarks were these statements:

"I attended one discussion. It was very educational and very interesting."
"There was a social hour with other widows. It was just lovely. The tone was so nice, you could just see how glad people were to be there."

Overall, only 34% of the clients who were interviewed about social gatherings arranged by the Center reported attending any. Seven percent said they weren't interested in such events. Sixteen percent said that the invitation had been for an inconvenient time, and 16% gave other reasons for not coming (too far, too expensive, too busy, etc.). By far the main reason why clients did not attend was because they had never received an invitation (27%). Many of the women expressed regret that they had never heard of such gatherings and said they definitely would have liked to attend if they had known about them.

The disappointment of a large portion of clients who had never received an invitation to a social event was raised by the evaluator as one of the early feedbacks of information from the follow-up interviews with clients. A suggestion was made that all clients be invited to some social event sponsored by the Center. The reasons why this was not done were explained in a letter from the director of the Center:

As a social service agency, one of our functions is to afford widows an opportunity to meet others with whom there is some possibility of forming a suitable acquaintanceship whether by virtue of location, similar backgrounds, life style, or special interests. The hope is that once having reached out to another individual or having someone reach out to her, a widow might then feel able to continue to relate to others in her community. But this requires thoughtful and very careful planning based on an intimate knowledge of each of our clients. It would, of course, be much easier to invite people indiscriminately on a rotating basis, but a wildly wholesale arrangement such as this could be a potentially destructive practice . . .

To invite people to this office on a nonselective basis simply because they are lonely and would like to have a place to come and talk with others would be to convert the Center into a clubhouse . . .

Our reactions to the suggestion that we invite all clients to come to lectures or social events are as follows:

1. Some of the discussions are inappropriate for many of our clients. To be of value to an individual the subject under consideration must be related in some way to that person's needs, background, and ability to benefit by the discussions . . .

2. In social contacts we have found that there are negative reactions on

the part of women who are asked to meet others on a totally different socio-economic level. They find it difficult to relate to each other if there is no basis for communication, no common interests and no possibility, for financial, geographical or other reasons, of engaging in the same education or recreational activities.

3. Unfortunately, there are among our clients a considerable number of mentally or emotionally disturbed women, some actual psychotics. We would avoid subjecting them or our other clients to possible incidents due to mental illness. For this and other reasons we would not issue blanket invitations to social events or even to general meetings, except under special circumstances.

The social activities at the Center are not the only means of helping women find new friends or activities, of course. Perhaps the primary means is making suggestions about things to do in their own neighborhoods, as described above in the chapter on individual counselling. Another means are the group therapy sessions. Here are some comments by caseworkers which show that the group therapy sessions are consciously used to help lonely widows make friends:

Evaluator: Is there any specific kind of widow or aspect of bereavement problems that are better dealt with in groups than individually?
Caseworker 1: Yes, I think the lonely widow, who has very few friends that she is compatible with at this particular time. Very often you hear a woman say, "Well, I have friends but they all have their husbands and I feel like an outsider." So there is something gained from being with another widow.
Evaluator: At what point is the widow typically ready for group discussions?
Caseworker 2: When she wants human relationships, I tell her that we have a little group of ladies that feel very much like herself. I let her know that we would like to include her. Sometimes, they respond "yes." Other times, "No, I don't want to talk to other women." When you get a negative reaction you have to be quick to tell her that it is natural at that time not to be wanting to talk to a whole group of people.
Evaluator: How do you decide whether or not to recommend that a woman join a discussion group for group therapy? I gather these are mainly for women who have emotional problems, some hostility or depression or whatever that needs working out. What kinds of problems or widows do you suggest it for?
Caseworker 3: Sometimes you suggest it for someone who is very isolated, who has very little outside contact. This may be a woman who really doesn't know how to make friends. In the small group session where she is able to discuss some of her fears and concerns, she may be able to come in contact with people in a nonthreatening situation, and from there move to a more social setting.

A cross-tabulation of the data from the follow-up interviews shows that there is a relationship between the number of group therapy sessions attended and the feeling that the Center had helped in finding new friends or activities. Among those clients attending three or more group therapy sessions, 38% said that the Center had helped in finding new friends and activities, compared to only 4% of those who attended no group therapy sessions.

DEALING WITH FAMILY PROBLEMS

In dealing with problems the widow has with children or other relatives, the Center is more likely to succeed in helping than to fail but it is also quite likely not to discover the existence of such a problem or not to deal with it at all. Thirty-nine percent of widows who had family problems at the time they went to the Center reported that the Center had helped the situation, whereas 25% said the Center had tried but failed to help, and 36% said that the Center had not tried to help with such problems. Part of the reason for this latter figure is that the policy of the Center is to refer its clients to existing family service agencies when they are available. As one caseworker put it, "If at all possible, if a family agency can be involved, I think that that is the proper place," rather than the Center, which has limited staff and no unique expertise in this problem area. A second caseworker added, "When the problem is one of a family nature, not truly one of bereavement, I feel that a family agency may be better able to handle it. When there is a school problem, for instance, they are better equipped to go out to the schools and make those visits that are necessary."

Those widows who report that the Center did help with family problems are most likely to credit the Center with helping their own insight into and acceptance of the situation, rather than with actually solving the problem. For example, one widow reported that she had been helped in her relations with her sons, one of whom had married a young woman whom she did not get along with, and the other who had moved out of his mother's home into his own apartment. In explaining what the Center did which helped her, the widow said, " It made me *feel* better. It made me understand more, although it couldn't change the situation."

DEALING WITH GOVERNMENT AGENCIES

Helping the client to deal with the Social Security Administration or other government agencies with which they might be having difficulties is a problem area in which the Center seems to have a high success rate. No widows who had such problems and mentioned them to the caseworker felt that the caseworker had not tried to solve the problem.

The staff tends to feel that they can be of real assistance with such problems for their less educated clients, who may be quite confused about the bureaucratic maze of forms and procedures. A caseworker says, "The lower group often has legitimate claims and we can help them obtain these. They would not know how to begin to fight for their claims without us . . ." Reports by the widows show that black women were especially likely to feel they had been helped by the Center with such problems (23% of all black clients reported being helped versus 7% of whites).

On the other hand, the caseworkers sometimes feel that their clients really have not been dealt with unfairly in the first place:

Well, I think that there is a limit to our intervention—I really do . . . A woman might bring in a long file of problems that she feels have been unresolved or not resolved to her benefit. Very often I feel the cases, when you get right down to rock bottom, have been very judiciously handled.

In other words, many of the cases which the widow perceives as being ones in which the counsellor tried, but failed to help, are perceived by the counsellor as not being legitimate problems, or not requiring her intervention.

MULTIPLE VISITS INCREASE EFFECTIVENESS

The more contact a client had with the Center, the more likely she was to feel that she had been helped, particularly with emotional problems, family problems, and finding new friends. This is a complex process to unweave, because first of all, those clients who received the most individual counselling sessions were those who were most likely to have *had* serious problems when they first came to the Center, in the areas of emotional aspects of bereavement, family problems, and finding new friends or activities. The same relationship occurs between attendance at three or more group therapy sessions and having had a serious problem of these types at the time they came to the Center. A second set of data shows that the more individual counselling sessions a widow had, then the more different problem areas she perceives the Center as having tried to help her with.

Finally, one finds that the proportion of widows who feel that the Center helped them with emotional problems, family problems, and finding friends increases substantially for those clients who had more than one private interview. Table 9.2 shows the relationship in detail. There is also a slight increase, with multiple visits, in the proportions helped with financial problems and dealing with government agencies. The same thing is generally true of attendance at group therapy sessions. The data show that the more group therapy sessions attended, the more likely the client was to feel that she had been helped with emotional problems, family problems, and finding new friends, but there is little relationship to helpfulness with other kinds of problems.

Looking at these figures in more detail for emotional problems, one can find that among those widows who had five or more personal consultations, there is a very good match between the proportions reporting serious emotional problems at the time they first came to the Center (76%) and the proportion reporting that the Center had helped them with emotional

Table 9.2

Clients Reporting Helpfulness of Center in Various Areas By Number of Private Interviews

| Problem Area | Number of Interviews | | | |
	One	Two-Four	Five or More	All
Emotional	42%	58%	80%	53%
Family	6%	12%	56%	15%
Finding a job	6%	5%	7%	6%
Living quarters	2%	10%	4%	5%
Finding friends	5%	11%	26%	9%
Government agencies	6%	9%	19%	9%
Financial matters	16%	13%	20%	16%
Total number	130	64	28	222

Source: Follow-up interviews.

problems (80%). (For this group, slightly more were helped than felt they had a serious problem in the first place.) There is more of a gap between need and help for those with from two to four visits (74% had serious emotional problems; 58% were helped).

We find a similar picture for problems with other family members. Among those widows with five or more visits, 50% reported having serious problems when they came, and 56% said they were helped with family problems. Among those with from two to four visits, 21% reported serious problems, and only 12% reported being helped. Help in finding friends also follows a similar pattern: with only one visit, the 5% helped come nowhere near the 29% reporting serious problems in this area. With five or more visits, 26% reported being helped, compared to the 43% who perceived this as a serious problem.

It is important to note again at this point that most of the clients included in the follow-up study did not have the advantage of multiple counselling sessions, since this had not been the policy of the Center at the outset. If clients during the third year of operation had been included, therefore, the overall figures for clients reporting that they had been helped would be closer to those in the "Five or more" visits column of Table 9.2.

OVERALL EVALUATION BY CLIENTS

Overall assessments of the helpfulness of the Center seem favorable, and also increase with the amount of contact with the Center. One classic criterion of what people think of a product or service is whether or not they would recommend it to their friends. The clients were asked, "Have you told any of your friends who are widows about the Widows Consultation Center?" Forty-two percent reported that they had, and 28% said they had included advice that the widowed friend go to the Center. Of course, not everyone has a widowed friend, so a second question was asked, "If a friend of yours were to *become* widowed, would you advise her to come to the Center? Why or why not?" The clients were almost unanimous in saying that they would advise a friend to go. Sixty-nine percent said, "Yes, they definitely thought the Center would help." Another 22% said that it would depend on what kind of problems the widowed friend had. Only 9% said that they would not recommend the Center to a friend.

A second question which was aimed at a total evaluation of the Center was, "Overall, would you say that the Widows Consultation Center was a great deal of help to you, of some help, or no help at all?" The assessments obtained from the answers to this question were favorable, but not quite as unanimous as the answers to the question on recommendation to a friend. Thirty-six percent said the Center had been "a great deal" of help; 33% of some help; 30%, no help.

Overall evaluations of the helpfulness of the Center by its clients became more favorable the more private interviews, group therapy sessions, or social activities attended. Table 9.3 shows the relationship for the number of private consultations with a caseworker. There is an especially large increase in the proportions reporting that the Center had been "a great deal of help" to them. For instance, less than a third of those clients who had only one or two private interviews felt that the Center had given them a great deal of help, compared to 79% of those who had five or more private consultation sessions. These findings support the feelings of the caseworkers that they can achieve much more success in helping their clients with a supportive casework process that extends over some period of time, rather than

Table 9.3

Percentage of Widows Recommending Center
(By Number of Private Interviews)

Number of Interviews	% Told friend	% Advised to come	% Definitely would advise	% Great deal of help
One	38	23	65	30
Two	33	27	67	27
Three	42	33	63	42
Four	58	50	75	50
Five or more	79	54	79	79
All	42	28	67	36

Note: The percentage columns tabulate responses to these questions.

1. Have you told any of your friends who are widows about the Widows Consultation Center?
2. Did you advise them to go to it or not?
3. If a friend of yours were to become widowed, would you advise her to come to the Center? Why or why not?
4. Overall, would you say that the Widows Consultation Center was a great deal of help to you, of some help, or no help at all?

Source: Follow-up interviews.

the kind of one-or-two visit-process which was usual during the first year of operation.

At this point, it might be appropriate to introduce some evidence about the validity of the reports about the effectiveness of the Center. Specifically, how well does the client's overall assessment of the Center as being a great deal of help, of some help, or of no help at all actually reflect the amount and impact of the advice and assistance they received? There is no way of determining this directly, but at least one can feel some increased confidence in the validity of the overall assessments when they are compared to the problem-by-problem assessments and found to be consistent. Those who say that the Center had helped them in each of the individual problem areas are also most likely to say that the Center had been "a great deal of help" overall.

So far we have been looking at evidence of a positive impact of the Center on its clients. Another consideration in evaluating its effectiveness is whether or not it is doing any harm to its clients or giving them advice which turns out to be poor when followed. A question included in the follow-up interview was, "Did you receive what you consider to be bad or inadequate advice from the Center in any area?" The results of this question are good. Only six widows, or 2% of those interviewed, said that they had received any bad or inadequate advice. We have no standard for comparison, but this seems remarkable.

VARIATIONS IN EFFECTIVENESS

It will be remembered that the target population for the Center is recently bereaved women, rather than long-term widows whose problems are those generally associated with poverty or aging. The follow-up interviews covered all clients, including older women who might have been widowed for many years and who were largely screened out or referred elsewhere after one consultation, in order to enable the Center to concentrate its limited resources on clients whom it is most equipped to help. It would naturally be expected that the assessments of the service received by these older clients would not be favorable, and this would lower the "average" assessment of the Center's helpfulness considerably.

The data bear out this line of reasoning and show that the assessment of the Center's helpfulness by the target population is much more favorable than the averages for all women who happened to come through the doors. Almost half (45%) of those clients who had been widowed for four years or longer at the time they first came to the Center reported that the Center did not try to give them help in any problem areas, in line with the policy described above. Conversely, women who had lost their husbands within the previous year were most likely to report for each of the problem areas that the Center had tried to help and had indeed been helpful, with the exceptions of finding a job or finding new living quarters.

The results are similar when looked at in terms of the age of the widow.

Those over sixty-five were most likely to report that the Center had not even tried to help them with any of their problems and least likely to report that the Center had been helpful with emotional problems, family problems, finding a job, or finding new friends or activities. On the other hand, not all older widows were turned away with no help at all. Clients over sixty-five were more likely than those under forty-five to report having been helped in dealing with government agencies (particularly Social Security, which is obviously age-related) and with help in managing finances.

In relation to income, women below the poverty level were most likely to report that the Center had been "no help at all," with 47% of women whose total household income was under $2,000 making this overall evaluation. There were no consistent differences in evaluations above this level. This indicates that as long as a woman is not so poor that this problem overshadows everything else, the Center is equally effective with women from all economic levels.

These differences discussed above indicate that if publicity and screening procedures of the Center could be developed so that inappropriate clients were not likely to receive appointments for private consultations,.the average "effective per client" or "effectiveness per interview" would be greatly improved.

There are slight differences in the overall ratings of the amount of help received associated with race, religion, and education. Thirty-eight percent of whites said they had received a great deal of help, compared with 27% of blacks. Forty-eight percent of Catholics said they had been helped a great deal, compared to 36% of Jewish clients and 26% of the Protestants. In relation to education, those women who had less than a high school education were most likely to feel they had been helped a great deal (46%), while those who had been to college were least likely to feel this way (31%). None of these differences seems large enough to be significant.

Another difference in the probable impact of the Center on its clients was pointed up by one of the caseworkers, who was reflecting on her experiences after more than two years of counselling widows:

Evaluator: In what kinds of cases do you feel you have the most success, and where do you seem to fail?
Caseworker: Well, I'll tell you one situation that is rather frustrating. When a member of the family brings a mother in, and usually it's the mother, sometimes it's the sister, and says she needs help. This woman says that she came because she wanted to please her son or daughter, but she really didn't come because she herself was motivated to come. These people are very, very hard to work with. In the first place, they are resistive, either verbally or psychologically, and they are not telling you that. Those cases are very difficult to handle.

This is another aspect of the screening process which might improve overall effectiveness. The Center could refuse to give an appointment unless the widow herself requests it.

Another striking difference in clients' assessments of the helpfulness of the Center occurs in relation to the skills and personality of the caseworker they happen to get. Three different caseworkers, including the director, served the clients in our study. One of the caseworkers was judged to have been helpful with emotional problems, family problems, and dealing with government agencies by larger proportions of her clients than were the other caseworkers. This is the caseworker who had the most experience at the Center at the time of the study. This worker's clients were also significantly more likely to give positive overall assessments of the helpfulness of the Center to them. (Fifty-two percent of all the widows she advised said the Center had been "a great deal of help" compared to only 18% for the least effective of the caseworkers.) This demonstrates the importance of having skilled counsellors and shows how the effectiveness of the Center or of any other counselling agency for widows will be greatly influenced by the individuals which are on its staff. The caseworkers also realize this, and feel that their effectiveness increases with the amount of experience they acquire in counselling widows. As one of them commented in an interview in October 1972:

For many women who come here, this is their last resort. I think it's fantastic how many women feel that they *have* been helped. You cannot be all things to all of these women, and maybe as our information and our skills continue to gather, we will be all the more effective. There is no question that all of us have to be open to refining our methods and continue to experiment [with helping techniques].

EFFECTIVENESS WITH RECENT WIDOWS WHO RECEIVE EXTENSIVE COUNSELLING

We have noted thus far that the target population for the Center is recent widows, and that their helping process changed over the first year toward a pattern of many counselling sessions. The follow-up study included twenty-two widows who had been widowed for three years or less at the time they first came to the Center and who received five or more counselling sessions. In this group, which may be considered the prototype of the kind of client group and service pattern that was developing, seventeen (77%) said that overall the Center had been "a great deal of help" to them; four said "some help"; and only one (5%) said "no help." This is very impressive and demonstrates that the Center can be very effective in helping recent widows deal with their problems.

SOME INDIVIDUAL CASES

The widows, their problems, and the help they were offered vary so much that it would be impossible to present any "typical" cases. But perhaps it could give the reader more of a feel for the actual case histories which lie behind the fragments we have summarized statistically in this chapter, if we looked at a few women whose overall reactions to the Center varied from "no help at all" to saying that it had been "a great deal of help."

One sixty-one-year-old woman who said that the Center had been "no help at all" had been widowed eight years when she came to the Center. She said she came because "I needed advice on financial matters. I needed work done on my teeth—they're all coming out. I wanted to find out if Social Security would pay." She saw a consultant once and did not attend any other activities. The consultant "called Medicaid and they said I was eligible, but when I went down there, they said 'No.'" A year later she still hadn't had her teeth done "because I can't afford it . . . It wasn't helpful because I wasn't eligible, not through any fault of theirs . . . She tried to be helpful but she couldn't. How can they help you financially?" But she added, "I thought it was wonderful even though they couldn't help me."

In this case, then, we see that the client was poverty-stricken and a long-time widow whose problem of financial need was not one the Center is set up to handle. It is no wonder that they were not of any help to her.

One case that resulted in an overall assessment that the Center had been "of some help" concerned a woman who had been widowed two years when she went to the Center. She said, "When I go, I take time off and leave my job, because it's helpful. I found even on entering the first time a warm, welcome feeling, no stiffness." This widow had one private consultation and attended several social activities subsequently. She went because she "wanted to talk in general," and emotional problems were serious for her. She said the consultant "was kind and sympathetic and I felt better after talking with her . . . You know there is someone you can go to talk to. She said I could call whenever I wanted to and I do call every now and again . . . " But emotional problems connected with bereavement are still "serious . . . There's a void and you can't fill it." Considering that this widow had what she called "serious" emotional problems, it is actually quite impressive that a single visit with a Center consultant helped at all.

Another widow who said that the Center was only "of some help" had been widowed two years when she came. She is quite well off, reporting about $70,000 in banks and investments and spending most of her time travelling around Europe and the United States. She came because she was having trouble with the probating of her husband's will in another state. She had one interview with a social worker and said, "She did extremely well. She has great warmth and understanding and was very eager to help."

She was referred to the Legal Referral Service, which informed her that she had to get a local lawyer in the state where the will was being probated. "Once I knew I had to get a lawyer there I was able to do it myself . . . I can't say it was a great deal of help to me because I didn't go to get a great deal, though I can see where it could be a great deal of help to others."

Almost all of the recent widows who had emotional problems related to bereavement and who went to the Center several times say it was "a great deal of help" to them. One such case is a woman who read a piece on the Center in the *New York Times* when she had been widowed only a month and called to make an appointment because she wanted to talk "about how miserable she was feeling." She had three individual consultations and attended several social activities. She said the consultant had been helpful with her emotional problems. "She let me talk and said my outlook for that short period was very good . . . She said I can call her anytime . . . [At the social activities] everything is positive . . . After the last discussion my whole outlook seemed to have been lifted . . . I see there are very many women like me and they go about their business and look nice, and that gives you an incentive to follow suit."

Another of those who feels she was helped a great deal is a woman who had been widowed six months when she first came to the Center. She relates that when she asked for an appointment, "I was so depressed and I wanted to talk to someone. I felt I couldn't adjust to being alone." She also had family problems; had lost her job; considered finding new friends and activities a serious problem ("Old friends don't seem close anymore. It's difficult to make new friends"); and had serious financial and health problems. She had six individual casework sessions and then began attending weekly group therapy sessions. She explains, "I feel they [the Center staff] offer you the warmth and understanding you need, which you can't get from family and friends. As much as they want to help, you feel you are annoying them . . . All the people at the agency are warn, understanding, and helpful . . . They try to explain how your feelings come about and that part of it is a natural part of bereavement . . . I found the group difficult to adjust to and I thought I'd rather be alone [with a caseworker] , but now I gain strength from the group and look forward to going."

Many longer-term widows who might be said to be suffering from "chronic bereavement and loneliness" have come back to the Center for the group therapy sessions or further individual sessions, and they also tend to be among those rating the Center as having been "a great deal of help." The final case we will look at fits in this category. Mrs. E. had been widowed five years when she first came to the Center. She had two individual consultations and then began attending group therapy sessions once a week. She said the consultant had helped her with her emotional problems and her family problems. "Just by talking and listening to me. By the time you left you felt better." The group had helped with her problems of needing new friends and activities. "I didn't want my old friends to see me that unhappy. . . We're becoming pretty good friends in the group at the Center . . . [in addition] I'm not as tense as I was. I'm not weeping and hysterical . . . [The Center has] created a friend. There is always a place I can go to when I feel very badly . . . They also help you understand yourself, which is very important. They can't take your troubles away, but they can help you face them better."

This last comment is probably the essence of what the Center feels it can do effectively.

A COST ANALYSIS

Anyone who is interested in beginning a new type of social service, such as one for widows, should be warned that a professional counselling service is not a shoestring operation. It takes a great deal of money, in addition to dedicated people, to get such an agency successfully operating.

The start-up costs of the Center were quite high. By December 1970, $9,500 had been spent for furniture and equipment, and another $500 for office design and layout of the space. In addition to such capital costs, the early months saw large fixed expenditures for rent and salaries, but a fairly small flow of clients. Any "cost per client visit" figure would look very high.

We will take a period near the end of the pilot phase as more typical of the costs and client load of the Center when it had reached its maturity (see Table 9.4). The period chosen is the first quarter of 1973, when capital expenses were very low and the Center was considered to be serving just about its capacity of clients. (The second quarter of 1973 had a slightly higher number of clients, but the rent was somewhat higher also, so the overall average would look similar.)

First, let's look at the expenditures. (An unknown portion of these, of course, may be attributable to the extensive record-keeping done by the caseworkers and the clerical staff in order to provide the data requested for the evaluation.) These totaled $32,800.

Balancing this were consultation fees received of $1,716, meaning that over $30,000 had to be met by outside donations of some sort—in this case, support by the Prudential Insurance Company. Although rent might be cheaper in other communities, the personnel costs for social workers, other professionals, and clerical support account for most of the costs, and these would be similar elsewhere.

Trying to quantify "services rendered" is quite a bit more difficult. It means that you must take the continuous efforts of the staff and somehow chop them up into "units of service," an arbitrary sort of operation. It would seem that the most logical way to measure service is from the point of view of the client, counting services actually received. Another consideration is that counting all contacts with clients equally, regardless of time spent or type of service given, would not make sense. Obviously a widow who is one of fifteen or twenty attending a Sunday program at the "Y" is not receiving as much service as the widow who has an hour or more of private counselling with her caseworker.

Table 9.4

Costs of Center Operation (First Quarter, 1973)

Item	Amounts	% of Budget
Staff salaries	$18,870	57
Fringe benefits and taxes	1,736	5
Outside consultants, services	6,272	19
(subtotal, personnel expenses)	($26,878)	(81)
Rent and electricity	4,168	13
Telephone	552	2
Office expenses (supplies, equipment purchase and rental, reference materials, etc.)	1,252	4
TOTAL	$32,850	100

Source: Widows Consultation Center financial reports.

The daily record forms kept by the caseworkers do not record the length of time spent in contact, but only the type of service activity (office consultation with client, intake call, collateral conference on behalf of client, etc.). Thus, the weighting or counting of even individual services must be somewhat arbitrary. (The problem of weighting of services would be solved if an agency used the system of recording all contacts in ten-minute units, as recommended in William McCurdy, *Daily Contact Reporting,* Family Service

Association of America, 1968. However, this would involve a somewhat more difficult task for the caseworker.) The system devised for this analysis starts with the premise that the most basic service of the Center is the individual consultation, scheduled as a one-hour appointment in the office. This will be called "one unit" of service, and all other types of services ranked in relation to it. A telephone contact with a client by her caseworker will be counted as a quarter unit, on the assumption that it takes about fifteen minutes on the average. Similarly, a telephone "intake" call with a new client will be counted as a quarter unit when it is handled by a caseworker or the director and involves the giving of information, referral, or setting of an appointment. A group discussion session or a social meeting, while lasting an hour or more, does not give each participant the undivided attention of the professional leader. Following the recommendation of the Center, each group discussion session attended will be counted as a half unit, and each social meeting as a quarter unit. Legal consultations and financial consultations, which usually involve the caseworker or director sitting in or conferring with the client about the advice given, will be counted as two units.

The coding of individual services rendered was done from the daily records kept by the caseworkers, on which they list the names of clients and the type of service given, with two coders reviewing each record independently. Many kinds of activities engaged in by the caseworkers and other staff members on behalf of the clients are not counted in this measure. Most importantly, collateral conferences, in which the caseworker talks to someone else about her client's problems, are omitted, as is all correspondence and record keeping. The hundreds of telephone and mail inquiries which are handled by the receptionist or which involve inquiries by parties who are not widows (such as newspapers), are not counted at all. These activities are all necessary in order for the staff to be of service to their clients, but they are not counted as service units. In addition there are undoubtedly many cases in which the busy staff member forgets to record a telephone call or other service contact on her daily record, and the free tickets to cultural events are all omitted. Our measure of benefits is probably an incomplete count of only the *major* types of services rendered to clients (see Table 9.5). Keeping these limitations in mind, the cost per unit of service was $38.00

The cost per unit could be brought down somewhat if collateral interviews and all other activities were counted, or if somewhat different weighting were used. If the average fees collected were forced to be more self-sufficient, this would surely discourage some clients. However, a tremendous gap between costs and fees collected would still remain.

Another way of simplifying the magnitude of the cost problem that must be dealt with is to look at the expenses for the quarter and to ask what fees would have to be charged to make the service self-sufficient. In the quarter we have been looking at, the Center would have had to collect $50 for each individual casework, financial, or legal consultation and $30 for each group discussion visit in order to generate enough income to assure covering its costs. (This would have resulted in $33,020 income for $32,850 in costs when the Center was booked nearly full. In the normally slower summer months the total revenue would not meet the fixed salary and rent

Table 9.5

Services by Widows Consultation Center

Service	X	Weight	=	Service units
Services, First Quarter 1973				
Individual Consultations (532)	X	1	=	532
Group Therapy Visits (189)	X	½	=	95
Legal Consultations (10)	X	2	=	20
Financial Consultations (5)	X	2	=	10
Social Activity Visits (133)	X	¼	=	33
Telephone Contacts, Old (463)	X	¼	=	116
Telephone Intakes (318)	X	¼	=	80
TOTAL 1650 client service contacts				886

Cost per unit = $37.00   Fees per unit = $1.94

Source: Social workers' daily record sheets and Widows Consultation Center summary reports on client flow. (Data totalled by two independent coders.)

costs even at this fee level.) Yet we have seen that most widows are financially unable to pay for this advice, and that even those who are relatively well off frequently balked at a $12.50 charge (about one fourth of the break-even charge). This is obviously a great problem, and once the Prudential's three-year grant ended, the Center was faced with a recurrent funding crisis.*

---

* This financial problem forced the closing of the Widows Consultation Center in January 1976.

COSTS OF ALTERNATIVE PROGRAMS

The Widows Consultation Centre in Winnipeg built upon the experiences of the New York Center but modified the service model in several important respects that resulted in greater economy. In my opinion, it provides a model which is much more financially feasible for the majority of communities than the original Widows Consultation Center.

First of all, rather than create a completely new and independent agency, it was decided, in consultation with United Way of Winnipeg personnel, that "it would be preferable that such a service should be developed as an expansion of an existing agency. The YWCA was thought to be most appropriate for this purpose because of its community acceptability and because it had already done some work in the area of programming for widows" (DeGraves, 1975).

As has been pointed out previously, existing family counselling agencies would be another possible kind of organization to which widows services could be "added on." The advantage of initiating a service for widows "under the wing" of an existing parent agency are obvious. There is no need for new and expensive quarters, for instance, and reception and clerical personnel can be shared, especially in the start-up period. (This alternative was not available to the Center in New York, where the Y's and existing family counselling agencies are sectarian.)

The Winnipeg Centre operates with only one professional social worker, who does all of the individual counselling and supervises the twice-a-month social programs, as well as supervising the three visiting widows in the widow-to-widow program and the group leader for their therapeutic discussion group. It is financed by a relatively modest grant by the Great West Life Assurance Company. (The grant is "matched" by the YWCA in space, staff support, etc.) Very detailed cost and service data are available for the widow-to-widow part of the service (DeGraves, 1975):

Length of pilot period: April 7-June 30, 1975 (12 weeks)
Number in sample: 118
Number who accepted service: 60 (51%)
Number who refused service: 39 (33%)
Unable to contact: 19 (16%)

Of the sixty widows who accepted service, twelve received one visit, and thirty-eight received more than one visit and/or telephone contact. There were 198 visits altogether.

Cost of service:
Salaries
    Visiting Widows $1,764.36 (458 hours)
    Director   234.11 (41 hours)

TOTAL	$1,998.47
Mileage	193.40
Books	6.00
TOTAL	$2,197.87
Projected annual cost (above × 4)	$8,791.48

The cost for each contact by the visiting widow was thus only $11.10. The projected service load would be about eight hundred such consultations by a visiting widow per year, compared with 116 such widows who received individual consultations with the professional social worker during the first year (66 in the office, 50 by telephone). In other words, this model is one in which individual counselling by a graduate social worker is available when needed, but the bulk of the client service will be given by trained and supervised (nonprofessional) visiting widows or in a group program context. It may be possible for such a program to be just as effective, judging from available feedback data. For instance, for the twenty-one Canadian widows who had agreed to see the visiting widow with no reservations, nineteen reported that overall the visiting widow had been moderately to very helpful, and none gave a negative answer. A definite advantage of this service model is that the costs are low enough so that they can all be covered by outside subsidies; no charges are made to widows for any of the services of the Canadian Centre.

SUMMARY AND CONCLUSIONS

Help with emotional problems stands out as the area in which widows feel that the Widows Consultation Center has been most helpful. Overall, 53% of widows who were questioned about this area said that the Center had been helpful to them. This is followed by help with financial matters (16% of those answering questions on this problem area reported they had been helped) and family problems (15%). In other problem areas, only a small proportion of clients felt that they had really been helped; 9% in dealing with government agencies; 9% in finding new friends or activities; 6% with finding a job; 5% with finding living quarters, and only 2% with problems of missing male companionship.

These evaluations by clients correspond to those of the staff, which felt that they were most effective in individual counselling on emotional problems, and least effective in trying to help widows cope with the shortage of suitable jobs and apartments in the metropolitan area.

The more contact a client had with the Center, the more likely she was to feel that she had been helped. The proportion of widows who felt that the Center helped them with emotional problems, family problems, finding friends, and dealing with government agencies increased substantially for those clients who had more than one private interview or who attended group therapy sessions.

Among the target group of clients—recently bereaved women—who had visited the Center several times, over three quarters reported that the Center had been "a great deal of help" to them. This figure probably represents best the Center's "success rate" by the end of the pilot period.

Another level of success is the institutional one. By the very fact of its existence, the Center has begun to stimulate attention to the plight of the widow.

The Center is serving as a focal point of a new awareness of how much the needs of widows have been neglected. In the New York City area, a number of psychiatric services, a local "Y," and the local Bar Association have all begun to cooperate with the Center's program. This positive reaction of parallel institutions is a measure of success that cannot be quantified, but it is just as impressive as the reactions of the widow-clients. More importantly, other communities, notably Winnipeg, have begun to look at what the Widows Consultation Center did and to set up similar services in their area.

On balance, we must conclude that the successes far outweigh the "failures." The latter mainly involved the structure of society—the difficulty of getting jobs for older, unskilled women, of getting better, cheaper housing in New York, of breaking out of isolation in a megalopolis. The Center cannot "solve" most of its clients' problems for them by resurrecting their dead husbands or finding them new ones, or by creating money or friends out of a void. If it can help the widow to understand and accept her situation, however, and to begin to build a more satisfying life, then it has succeeded.

Although there are many ways in which the Widows Consultation Center could have further improved its services to widows and lowered the costs involved, the most important thing to be emphasized is that the Center is a very successful pilot operation. It deserves to be supported as a permanent social service in the New York City area, and to be emulated as a prototype for similar services in other communities. It is hoped that this book will help social service agencies in other communities to borrow and adapt features of the programs developed by the Center during its pilot phase, while modifying them to fit the level of client demand and available financial and social resources in their own communities.

APPENDIXES

A. SOME ORGANIZATIONS OFFERING SERVICES TO WIDOWS

Eve—Women's Center
Kean College
Union, New Jersey

One-day conferences and weekly group workshops specifically for widows and widowers. Educational, vocational and personal counselling for all clients.

Widows Consultation Centre
447 Webb Place
Winnipeg, Manitoba
R3B 2P2 Canada

Individual counselling; widow-to-widow program; group sessions; social activities.

Widowed Persons Service
1909 K Street, N. W.
Washington, D. C.

Widow-to-widow program; group discussions.

Widow's Information and Consultation Service
1005½ S. W. 152nd Street
Seattle, Washington 98166

Widow-to-widow program; group discussions.

The Widowed to Widowed Program
6655 Alvarado Road
San Diego, California 92120

A program for the newly widowed. Services include visits by widowed persons; small discussion groups; twenty-four-hour hotline; assistance in locating other widows in a neighborhood.

Laboratory of Community Psychiatry
Harvard Medical School
Cambridge, Massachusetts

Discussion groups for widows and widowers.

ORGANIZATIONS WITH A RELIGIOUS ORIENTATION

NAIM Conference
National Office
109 North Dearborn
Chicago, Illinois 60602

According to director, NAIM helps widows and widowers, "psychologically, financially, legally and spiritually." Monthly meetings; social activities, including family parties and picnics. Membership is limited to Catholics and spouses of deceased Catholics.

THEOS (They Help Each Other Spiritually)
11609 Frankstown Road
Pittsburgh, Pennsylvania 15235

Nondenominational Christian group for the newly bereaved young and middle-aged person.

Jewish Widow-Widower Club
2 Concord Avenue
Belmont, Massachusetts 02178

Widows and widowers meet monthly to discuss problems or listen to speakers offering information on travel, investment, housing, etc.

B. PROCEDURES AND PROBLEMS IN EVALUATING THE CENTER

This decade has seen the appearance of a number of publications in the area of "evaluation research," the effort to systematically apply social science research methods to the evaluation of action programs set up to help solve social problems. Evaluation research is thus one area in which social scientists can be of direct aid in setting public policy about social welfare services.

An excellent primer on the problems that are likely to arise in the course of an evaluation effort and the "conventional wisdom" that has been developed thus far is Carol Weiss's *Evaluation Research: Methods of Assessing Program Effectiveness* (1972). Had her work been available when the research reported here was designed, some of the problems encountered might have been foreseen and dealt with more wisely. There are also a number of readers which have appeared recently, including Caro's *Readings in Evaluation Research* (1971) and Weiss's *Evaluating Action Programs* (1972). As the fine twenty-four page bibliography in the latter volume shows, however, there is a lot more published material about the conceptual and methodological issues which arise in evaluation research, treated in the abstract, than there are case studies which illustrate the fact that evaluation research is often an essentially political process of conflict and bargaining among the researcher, the staff members whose program is under scrutiny, and the funding agencies. To paraphrase a famous aphorism, the sociologist who is not aware of previous research problems and mistakes is condemned to repeat them. This appendix is an attempt to relate some of the specific research procedures and research problems that arose in evaluating the three-year pilot project phase of the Widows Consultation Center, related from the obviously biased position of the evaluator.

NEGOTIATING RESEARCH PROCEDURES

The fundamental problem encountered was how to mesh the often conflicting demands of evaluation research and social service. If the evaluator set up a rigorous experimental research design which suited her purposes, the results might very well have been disgruntled staff and outraged clients who felt that they were being used as guinea pigs rather than being helped. If the social workers were able to proceed completely in the manner they found most satisfying, it would exclude the systematic collection of data needed for evaluation and the potentially disruptive monitoring of their work with clients.

The basic design worked out for the evaluation was a "before" and "after" measure of the clients, with observation and monitoring of the various services that were developed. Specifically, the plan was for the caseworker to administer an extensive set of questions to the widow about her problems as part of the intake interview. The same questions could be included later in a follow-up interview with clients after several months, and the changes measured. The amounts and kinds of services received from the Center and the clients' assessments of their helpfulness could be used to assess the "cause" of any changes. Added to this would be direct observation of such things as group discussion sessions and intensive interviews with staff in order to observe what kinds of techniques seemed to work. However, staff resistance to the kind of interference with their work implied by these elaborate plans precluded their complete implementation.

There is always a good deal of stress and strain when professionals from different fields must cooperate in a joint research undertaking, and the differences in values between social workers, oriented toward service, and a sociologist, oriented toward research, are inevitably going to result in clashes over priorities. As Mann (in Caro, 1971) notes about such evaluations, "The institute staff tend to consider the researcher as a necessary evil, who must be tolerated for a time, but whose prime function seems to be to make their difficult life even more complex by giving them more forms to fill out . . ."

Difficulties began with the design of a case history form. From the point of view of the evaluator, several standardized questions on the severity of various problems were desired, with the idea of repeating these same questions in a follow-up interview. The staff of the Center found this totally unacceptable on the grounds that it would interfere with their ability to help clients. Here is an account of a visit to the Center during its first month of operation (July 1970) when the evaluator discovered that the structured interview guide which had initially been designed for use during a client's first visit was not being used at all. (This account was written immediately after the discussion, with the omissions and simplifications that such recall always involves.)

Evaluator: Why don't you even *try* to use the interview guide?
Caseworker: I will cooperate with your research only if it does not interfere with the service I can offer my clients. After an hour and a half or so of talking with me about their problems, you cannot expect the client to answer all of these questions.
Evaluator: When do you think you could fit these questions in?
Caseworker: I brought this up with one woman I have seen, and I really don't know. Perhaps, after we have seen the client and helped her, we could ask her if she wouldn't be willing to come to the Center some day and help us by completing a short questionnaire.
Evaluator: No, no, this is totally unacceptable. I've told you that we need to get a survey of the woman's problems and feelings before you have helped her. And it must be done for all clients, not just for those who feel grateful enough to make a special trip to the Center to fill out a questionaire.
Caseworker: I have heard all that before.
Evaluator: [pleading] Please, won't you try to incorporate the questions into the initial long interview?
Caseworker: It isn't a matter of trying; I would be embarrassed to ask these questions. I do not intend to ruin the reputation of the Center by subjecting widows to questions that they might not think are applicable to them. What is discussed by the widows must come from *them;* must be what they want to talk about. The Center must not try to impose questions on its clients that they do not bring up of their own accord in the course of an interview.

What is obvious in retrospect is the emotionality and the clash of priorities among the parties involved.

A meeting was called at which the staff and the evaluator went over the whole form, question by question. Such a meeting among all interested parties is recommended to others as a way of dealing with apparent impasses between researcher and practitioners. It produces a group consensus of one sort or another, which then does not seem to be "imposed" on the staff by the outside evaluators. Although the idea of a consensus-seeking meeting seems to be a good one for restoring the momentum of an evaluation effort, unfortunately the result of the lengthy bargaining process turned out in practice to be a very unsatisfactory compromise. The case history form settled upon was time-consuming and annoying to the caseworkers, and also unsatisfactory to the evaluator, because it included no questions with standardized wording. Moreover, when coded, the case history form produced a large number of "no answers" because the caseworker had not thought a question propitious at the time of the intake interview. In addition the pages of material produced for the open-ended questions to the caseworkers (parts M, N, and O) were almost impossible to code for computer processing. As a result of this experience, it is recommended that in the future, whenever funds permit, separate interviews or questionnaires at the time of intake be conducted for research purposes, rather than trying to make the social worker's intake interview serve both the diagnostic/record keeping functions of a case history for the agency's purposes, and as "baseline" measures for research purposes.

In addition, future evaluators would do well to establish regular (perhaps bi-monthly) meetings with all staff to review the progress of the evaluation effort and to revise procedures which do not work out well.

FOLLOW-UP INTERVIEW PROCEDURES

A letter from the director of the Center asking for the clients' cooperation in the study included a postcard addressed to the Center on which the widow could indicate that she did not wish to be interviewed. After two or three weeks, those who had not returned the postcard were contacted by telephone or mail by an interviewer in order to set up an appointment. Whenever possible, an appointment was made for the interviewer to go to the widow's home and interview her in person. A few clients requested the suggested option of being interviewed at the Center rather than at home.

Telephone interviews were requested with those clients who lived outside of New York City (for whom travel time would have made a personal interview expensive) or in Harlem (the white interviewer assigned to Manhattan felt that it was unsafe for her). In addition, a client who refused to make an appointment for a personal interview was asked if she would agree to a ten or fifteen minute telephone interview. If the client refused a telephone interview, she was then requested to answer just a few questions on her overall reactions to the Center (an "incomplete" telephone interview).

The telephone interview does not include three sets of questions which were asked in the personal interviews: those on finances, relations with men, and current emotional state. It was felt that the telephone interview situation would not generate enough rapport to insure that questions in these areas would not result in the widow's breaking off the interview or becoming upset. Hindsight based on reports from the interviewers suggests that this information could have been obtained over the telephone in many cases, and that whether or not to include such questions should have been left to the discretion of the interviewer.

Table A.1 is a frequency distribution of the time periods which had elapsed between a client's initial visit to the Center and the completion of a follow-up interview.

There was a strong relationship between the number of visits to the Center and the likelihood of completing a personal interview as shown in Table A.2.

Table A.1

Distribution of Time Lapse between Initial Visit and Follow-up
Interview

	Number	%
4-6 months	39	16
7-9 months	55	22
10-12 months	46	18
13-15 months	75	30
16 or more months	35	14
TOTAL	250	100

Source: Case history records and follow-up interviews.

Table A.2

Total Number of Visits to the Center
(By Outcome of Follow-up Interview Attempt)

	Personal interview	Phone, incomplete	Phone, incomplete	Other	Total	
One	27%	21%	9%	42%	100%	(N=335)
Two	38%	26%	10%	26%	100%	(N= 39)
Three to Five	50%	18%	––	32%	100%	(N= 22
Six or more	87%	––	––	13%	100%	(N= 15)
TOTAL	32%	19%	8%	41%	100%	(N=439)

Source: Widows Consultation Center case history records and face sheet of follow-up
interview forms.

A purely research interview would be concerned with getting "facts" and leaving. During the first pretests, I found that widows tended to view the interviewer in the role of a kind of "extension service" from the Center. What had to be done in this interview situation was to make sure that the interviewers would be supportive and helpful whenever possible, but not take on a counselling role for which they might not be trained. It is probable that evaluation research involving interviews with clients of any type of social service might encounter similar types of problem situations and similar opportunities to serve as a liaison with the caseworkers when a client seems to need more help.

C. INSTRUMENTS USED IN DATA COLLECTION

The text of instruments used in data collection is included in this appendix; however, the considerable amounts of space which were left for answers have been omitted.

The Case History Form was filled out by the caseworker when the client first visited the Widows Consultation Center, and short supplementary reports were added after additional counselling sessions. The evaluation research staff coded this information (using copies from which the name, address, and all other identifying information had been removed) and stored it on punched IBM cards.

The Suggested Interview Request Format was used when clients whose telephone numbers were known were called and asked to grant a follow-up interview. Those whose telephone numbers were unknown were reached by mail or by personal visit without an appointment (unless they had already declined an interview).

The Record of Widows Consultation Center Follow-up Interview Efforts was returned to the Center. There, the name and address were whited out and the client's identification number was written on this form and on the first page of the Interview Report Form (if one had been filled out). Neither the coders of the interview information nor I had any way of knowing the identity of individuals. The identification number was the means of linking this coded keypunched data with the case history record.

The items in question 57 of the Personal Interview, Widows Consultation Center Clients, were borrowed from a questionnaire developed at the Harvard Medical School by Dr. Robert Weiss. I am very grateful to him for sharing his questionnaire with me at an early stage in his research.

I encourage others to borrow freely from these instruments in evaluating similar programs, provided only that they acknowledge the source and send a copy of the results. Coding instructions are available on request.

1. CASE HISTORY FORM

A. Application no.
Name
Client's date of birth
Home address

Home telephone
Business address

Business telephone
Race
Place of birth
Date of marriage

Husband's name
Date of birth
Place of birth
Date of death
Husband's occupation

Name of relative or friend through whom you can be reached
Relationship

Name
Address

Telephone number

B. Referred by

Date
Interviewer initials
Typist initials

C. Client's request

D. Family structure (Include everyone living with client plus other members of immediate family)
Relationship   Year of
to client   Name and address   birth   Occupation

E. Housing
Apartment
House.
Number of rooms
(Check one)
Own   Resale value
Rent   Monthly rental
Is widow considering change in housing arrangement?

F. Client's occupation
Present
Previous

Describe job. How long employed? Is she happy with this position or would she like something else?

If not employed, is she looking for employment? What kind of position?

(continued)

(1. Case History Form continued)

G. Volunteer service

H. Client's education School(s) attended last
   Degree(s) or certification
   Adult classes

I. Client's health
   Present, recent illnesses, operations

   Health insurance coverage

J. Finances
   1. Amount of life insurance on husband
      Who was the beneficiary?
      How were life insurance proceeds used?
   2. Amount of life insurance on self
   3. Social Security income per month
   4. Pension income per month
   5. Assets   Total Amount   Any monthly income from this source?
      Savings accounts
      Stocks or corporate bonds
      Government bonds
      Other (What?)
   6. Other source of income?
   7. Widow's total present monthly income
   8. Household total monthly income
   9. Debts (total amounts and type)
   10. What was the total annual family income during the last two years the husband was alive?
   11. Is there anyone who has helped with financial arrangements since the husband's death, such as life insurance agent, banker, lawyer, or relative? Who?

K. Religious affiliations
   Church, synagogue, temple

   Has applicant consulted religious leader since husband's death?

   Active-inactive?

L. Current leisure activities and their frequency

M. Circumstances surrounding husband's death and applicant's reaction

N. Current emotional state

O. Evaluation of situation and the widow's resources for dealing with her problems

P. Checklist of problem areas
   (Explore the extent to which each of the following is a problem area. If a subject has already been covered, fill in from this previously acquired data.)

   1. Living alone
      No problem   Problem   Describe

   2. Problems with in-laws
      No problem   Problem   Describe

   3. Problems with children
      No problem   Problem   Describe

(continued)

(1. Case History Form continued)

4. Problems with other relatives
   No problem Problem   Describe

5. Relations with old friends
   No problem Problem   Describe

6. Finding some new friends
   No problem Problem   Describe

7. Relations with men
   No problem Problem   Describe

8. Relationship with the children (if any)
   No problem Problem   Describe

9. Settling the estate
   No problem Problem   Describe.

10. Financial matters, such as income tax, Social Security, or investments
    No problem Problem   Describe

Q. Disposition _____

R. Fee _____

S. Supplementary reports _____

2. SUGGESTED INTERVIEW REQUEST FORMAT

Hello, Mrs. ....?

My name is........., and I am calling you concerning the Widows Consultation Center. You should have received a letter recently from the Center, explaining that they would appreciate your co-operation in finding out if the Center has helped you. (Pause for affirmation) I would like to make an appointment to come to your home and talk with you about your experiences with the Center. Would.........be convenient for you?

3. RECORD OF WIDOWS CONSULTATION CENTER FOLLOW-UP INTERVIEW EFFORTS

Case Number   Address   Tel. no.

Name   Interviewer

Date of WCC visit   Date letter sent

Telephone Contacts

Date   Purpose   Response

Appointment made for?   Was appointment kept?

If interview refused: reason for refusal

Is there any indication that respondent has married?

If applicable:

New telephone number   Name of friend or relative

New address   Telephone number

4. PERSONAL INTERVIEW
WIDOWS CONSULTATION CENTER CLIENTS

Case no.   Date   Interviewer

Time begun   Time ended

Hello, Mrs.   I am   and I have come to talk to you about your experiences related to the Widows Consultation Center.

Before we begin, let me assure you that the information that you give me will be held in confidence, and of course, if there is some particular question that you'd rather not answer, just tell me and we will skip it.

First of all, according to the records of the Widows Consultation Center, you first came to the office in Manhattan during (month) (year)   Is that correct?   Yes   No.

1. When did you first become a widow?   year.
Then, when you first came to the Center, you had been widowed for   , and now you have been widowed for

(continued)

(4. Personal Interview continued)

2. Do you remember how you first heard of the Widows Consultation Center?

3. Thinking back to then, do you remember if you called the Center for information or went directly to the Center without calling first?

   Called   Came in person

4. What sort of things did you want to talk to the Widows Consultation Center about when you first contacted it?

5. What were your initial feelings or impressions when you contacted the Center for an interview?

   Did the person who talked to you make you feel that the Center could help you?

6. Do you remember the name of the consultant with whom you spoke when you came for an interview?

7. Would you have preferred to have the interview handled differently in any way?

8. All together, how many times did you have a *private* interview with one of the ladies?

   a. (If more than one interview) Were these all with the same person?

9. a. Did you attend any group discussion session?
   b. (If No) Why not?

   c. (If Yes) How often?

   d. Who was your group discussion leader?

   e. Tell me about your experiences.

   f. Do you have any suggestions about how the group discussions might be improved?

10. Which if any, of the social activities sponsored by the Center did you attend?

   a. If none: Why not?

   b. If any: How did you feel about this (these) activity?

   I would like to go over some problems of concerns that you might have had when you came to the Center and find out to what extent these problems have been solved, and if you have any new problems. I will go over some possible areas in which many widows have problems one at a time, since this is the only way to make sure that nothing is left out. For each of them, I am going to ask you to tell me if you would call it a serious problem, somewhat of a problem, or not a problem at all.

   If respondent has been widowed more than five years, skip to question 13.

11. How about becoming emotionally adjusted to your widowhood? Would you say that this was a serious problem for you when you came to the Center, somewhat of a problem, or not a problem at all?

   (continued)

(4. Personal Interview continued)

Serious   Somewhat of a problem   Not a problem

If serious or somewhat, probe for nature of problem.

If yes:

a. Did the consultant with whom you spoke or anyone else at the Center talk to you about it or do anything to try to help you to feel better?

b. If yes, what did they do?

c. Was this helpful or not?

d. Do you think there is anything the Center could do to to be of more help to widows in dealing with the emotional problems of bereavement?

e. Has anything else happened to you in the meantime to help or hinder your emotional adjustment to widowhood?

If yes, what?

12. (Ask all) How about the way you feel *now*—would you say that at the present time emotional upset connected with being a widow is a serious problem for you, somewhat of a problem, or not a problem at all?

Serious   Somewhat of a problem   Not a problem

If serious or somewhat, probe for nature of problem.

Now, let's turn to a different problem area.

13. How about relationships with your children or with any other relatives? When you first came to the Center, was this a serious problem for you, somewhat of a problem, or not a problem at all?

Serious   Somewhat of a problem   Not a problem

If serious or somewhat, probe for nature of problem.

If yes:

a. Did your consultant or anyone at the Center do anything to try to help you work out these problems with your _____ ?

If yes, what?

b. Did this improve the situation or not?

c. Do you think there is anything the Center could do to to be more helpful to widows who have problems with children or other family members?

d. Did anything else happen that affected your relationship?

If yes, what?

14. (All) At the present time, would you say that you have serious problems in your relationship with any family members, somewhat of a problem, or no problem at all?

Serious   Somewhat of a problem   Not a problem

If serious or somewhat, probe for nature of problem.

Now, looking at your employment situation.

15.

a. Do you have either a volunteer or a paid position at the present time?

(continued)

(4. Personal Interview continued)

None   Volunteer   Paid

b. (If job) What is your job?

c. Do you work part time or full time?

   Part time   Full time

d. Did you have this same job at the time you came to the Center?

16. When you first came to the Center, was finding a good (better) job a serious concern for you, somewhat of a problem, or not a problem at all?

   Serious   Somewhat of a problem   Not a problem

If serious or somewhat, probe for nature of problem.

If yes:

a. What kind of position were you looking for?

b. Did anyone at the Center try to help you find a job?

c. Did this actually help you in getting a job?

d. Is there anything that happened aside from the Center's efforts that has changed your job situation?

If yes, what?

e. Is there anything that the Center could do to be of more help to widows who need jobs?

If yes, what?

17. What about now? Would you say that concerns about a (your) job are a serious problem for you, somewhat of a problem, or not a problem at all?

   Serious   Somewhat of a problem   Not a problem

If serious or somewhat, probe for nature of problem.

18. When you came to the Center, was finding a more suitable place to live a serious concern for you, somewhat of a problem, or not a problem at all?

   Serious   Somewhat of a problem   Not a problem

If serious or somewhat, probe for nature of problem.

If yes:

a. Did anyone at the Center try to help you find a more suitable place to live?

b. Was the situation improved?

c. Is there anything that happened aside from the Center's efforts that helped you find a more suitable place to live?

If yes, what?

19. What about now? Would you say that concern about suitable living quarters is a serious problem for you, somewhat of a problem, or not a problem at all?

   Serious   Somewhat of a problem   Not a problem

(continued)

(4. Personal Interview continued)

If serious or somewhat, probe for nature of problem.

Now, let's turn to your leisure time activities.

20. During the past seven days how many people have you visited or had as guests in your home? _____ number

21. What else do you do with your leisure time at present?

    How often?

    Anything else?

22. How many close friends do you have at present?

23. Back when you came to the Center, were relations with old friends or finding *new* friends or activities to keep you occupied a serious concern for you, somewhat of a problem, or not a problem at all?

    Serious   Somewhat of a problem   Not a problem

    If serious or somewhat, probe for nature of problem.

    If yes:
    a. Did anyone at the Center try to help you find new friends or activities?

    b. Was the situation improved?

    c. Is there anything that happened aside from the Center's efforts that helped you to find new friends or activities?

    If yes, what?

24. Would you say that right now finding new friends or activities is a serious problem for you, somewhat of a problem, or not a problem at all?

    Serious   Somewhat of a problem   Not a problem

    If serious or somewhat, probe for nature of problem.

25. When you first came to the Center, was dealing with Social Security or other government agencies a serious concern for you, somewhat of a problem, or not a problem at all?

    Serious   Somewhat of a problem   Not a problem

    If yes:
    a. Which agencies?

       What kind of problems?

    b. Did anyone at the Center try to help you deal with Social Security or other government agencies?

    c. Was the situation improved?

    d. Is there anything that happened aside from the Center's efforts that helped you to deal with Social Security or other government agencies?

       If yes, what?

26. What about now? Would you say that dealing with Social Security or other government agencies is a serious problem for you, somewhat of a problem, or not a problem at all?

    Serious   Somewhat of a problem   Not a problem
    (continued)

(4. Personal Interview continued)

If serious or somewhat, probe for nature of problem and which agencies.

27. What about managing your money or making ends meet—would you say you were seriously concerned about your financial position when you came to the Widows Consultation Center, somewhat concerned, or money matters were not a problem at all?

    Serious   Somewhat concerned   Not a problem

If serious or somewhat, probe for nature of problem.

Since finances are often a widow's most serious long-term problem, we'd like to go into this in some detail in order to gain more understanding of how widows manage to get along.

28. (Ask only if widowed five years ago or less) Here is a card with income categories. Looking at List I, on the left, could you tell me the letter of income category in which your family's yearly income fell before your husband died—say the two years right before his death. (Show List I) Letter

29. Was there any life insurance on your husband? ... Yes ... No

(If Yes)
a. What category in List I approximates the total amount of life insurance your husband had?

b. Who was the beneficiary?

c. How were the proceeds of the life insurance used?

30. Other than life insurance, what else did your husband leave you? (Probe for amounts by showing List I)

House	Savings
Car	Investments
Real estate	

31. Did you have any debts or medical bills to pay? What amount? (Show List I)

32. How about your financial situation now?

a. Do you yourself have any income from a job?

    (If yes) What category in List II on the right, does your monthly wage or salary fall into?

33. What is your monthly Social Security income? (List II)

34. What is your monthly income from pension funds? (List II)

35. Going back to List I, roughly how much do you have in savings accounts at the present time? (List I)

36. Do you have any investments—Types and Amounts?

    Type 1   Amount from List I
    Type 2   Amount from List I

37. Do you have any other sources of income?

    Type 1   Monthly amount from List II
    Type 2   Monthly amount from List II

38. Putting everything together, then, what is your total monthly income, before taxes, at the present time? *(continued)*

(4. Personal Interview continued)

List II   (amount)

39. Do you have any life insurance on yourself now?
List I   (amount)

40. What about health insurance—how are you covered?

If Medicare, do you have anything besides Medicare?

41. Do you have any outstanding debts now?

Type 1   Amount (List I)
Type 2   Amount (List I)

42. Did the Center do anything to try to help you with financial matters?

     Yes   Probe for what

     No

43. Did you find that this was helpful to you or not?

44. Has anything else happened since you first came to the Center to improve you financial condition or to make it worse?

If yes, what?

45. Right now, would you say that money matters are a serious problem for you, somewhat of a problem, or not a problem at all?

     Serious   Somewhat of a problem   Not a problem

If serious or somewhat, probe for nature of problem.

46. Turning to a more personal area, have you done any dating during the last six months or so?

47. Back when you first came to the Center, was lack of male companionship or sexual fulfillment a serious problem for you, somewhat of a problem, or not a problem at all?

     Serious   Somewhat of a problem   Not a problem

If serious or somewhat, probe for nature of problem.

If yes:
a. Did anyone at the Center try to help you with the problem of lack of male companionship?

b. Was the situation improved?

c. Is there anything that happened aside from the Center's efforts that helped to improve the situation?

     If yes, what?

48. What about now? Would you say that the lack of male companionship or sexual fulfillment is a serious problem for you, somewhat of a problem, or not a problem at all?

     Serious   Somewhat of a problem   Not a problem

If serious or somwhat, probe for nature of problem.

49. Are there any other problems we haven't talked about that you needed help with when you came to the Center or that you have a problem with now?

If yes, what are they?

(continued)

(4. Personal Interview continued)

Problem 1

Nature of problem:

a. Did your consultant or the Center do anything to help you with this problem?

If yes, what?

b. Was the situation improved?

c. Has anything else happened to affect the problem?

If yes, what?

d. Is it a serious problem, somewhat of a problem, or not a problem now?

Serious   Somewhat of a problem   Not a problem

If serious or somewhat, probe for nature of problem.

Problem 2

Nature of problem:

a. Did your consultant or the Center do anything to help you with this problem?

If yes, what?

b. Was the situation improved?

c. Has anything else happened to affect the problem?

If yes, what?

d. Is it a serious problem, somewhat of a problem, or not a problem now?

... Serious ... Somewhat of a problem ... Not a problem

If serious or somewhat, probe for nature of problem.

50. Overall, what was the most helpful thing that the Widows Consultation Center did for you, if anything?

51. Did you receive what you consider to be bad or inadequate advice from the Center in any area? (If yes: probe for detailed description)

52. Have you told any of your friends who are widows about the Widows Consultation Center?

Yes   No

If yes, did you advise them to go to it or not? Why?

Did they go?   Why or why not?

53. If a friend of yours were to *become* widowed, would you advise her to come to the Center? Why or why not?

54. a. Do you remember if you paid a consultation fee to the Center for any of your visits?

b. (If yes) How much did you pay?

c. Did you feel that this was a fair amount, considering your circumstances, too much, or too little?

(continued)

(4. Personal Interview continued)

55. Overall, would you say that the Widows Consultation Center was a great deal of help to you, of some help, or no help at all?

56. Do you have any criticisms of the way the Center is operated which we have not talked about?

57. I am going to read you some statements that many widows have made. I would like you to tell me how often in the *last month* you have had thoughts or experiences like these—not at all, occasionally, or most of the time.

Not at all   Occasionally   Most of the time

1. Nobody cares about me
2. No one really understands how I feel
3. I feel some how it was my fault that my husband died
4. I can't seem to sleep. I lie awake for hours after I go to bed
5. There doesn't seem to be any reason to go on living
6. I'm worried I might have a nervous breakdown
7. I'm going to be able to work things out
8. I am finding some new meanings and purposes in life

58. That is all the questions I have to ask. Is there anything we have not talked about that you think I should have asked?

Thank you very much for your cooperation. I certainly do appreciate the time you've taken to talk to me.

5. INTERVIEWER REPORT FORM

1. How cooperative was the respondent? (Did she seem to enjoy the interview or to resent it? Do you think she was candid?)

2. Did she get emotionally upset or cry at any point?

3. Are there any questions which she had difficulty answering or refused to discuss?

4. Describe the quality of the living quarters (apartment or house size, number and quality of furnishings, external appearance of building, etc.).

5. Condition and cleanliness of living quarters (broken furniture, stains or rips, disarray, dust and dirt, etc.).

6. What is your estimate of the neighborhood?
   high income   stable middle class
   working class or mixed (somewhat deteriorated)
   slum

7. Thumbnail sketch or other comments.

REFERENCES

Adams, Bert
1968   "The Middle-Class Adult and His Widowed or Still-Married Mother." *Social Problems* 16 (Summer): 50–59.

Albaum, Martin, Ronald Miller, and John Considine
1965   *Life Insurance Beneficiaries: Widows under Fifty.* The Prudential Insurance Company, unpublished report.

Berardo, Felix M.
1968   "Widowhood Status in the United States: Perspective on a Neglected Aspect of the Family Life Cycle." *The Family Coordinator* 17: 191–203

Bureau of the Census
1972   "Population Characteristics, Marital Status and Living Arrangements, March 1972." *Current Population Reports* Series P-20: no. 242.

1974   "Marital Status and Living Arrangements, March 1974." *Current Population Reports* Series P-20: no. 271.

Caine, Lynn
1974   *Widow.* New York: Wm. Morrow & Co., Inc.

Caro, Francis (ed.)
1971   *Readings in Evaluation Research.* New York: Russell Sage Foundation.

CRUSE: The Organization for Widows and Their Children
1968   "The Work of CRUSE, Annual Report, 1967–68." Richmond, Surrey, England.

DeGraves, Diane
1975   "The Widow-to-Widow Program" and "The Widows Consultation Centre"; mimeographed reports available from the Widows Consultation Centre, 447 Webb Place, Winnipeg, Manitoba.

Durkheim, Emile
1951   *Suicide.* Glencoe: The Free Press (first published 1897).

Freud, Sigmund
1917   "Mourning and Melancholia." *Collected Papers.* New York: Basic
        Books, 1959, 4: 152–170.

Glick, Ira O., Robert S. Weiss, and C. Murray Parkes
1974   *The First Year of Bereavement.* New York: John Wiley.

Life Insurance Agency Management Association (LIAMA)
1970   *The Widows Study.* Volume I, The Onset of Widowhood. Volume
        II, Adjustment to Widowhood: The First Two Years.

Lindemann, Erich
1944   "The Symptomatology and Management of Acute Grief."
        American Journal of Psychiatry 101: 141–148.

Lopata, Helena Znaniecki
1969   "Loneliness: Forms and Components." *Social Problems* 17 (Fall):
        248–262.

1972   "Role Changes in Widowhood: A World Perspective," in Cowgill
        and Holmes (eds.), *Aging and Modernization.* New York: Apple-
        ton-Century-Crofts, pp. 275–304.

1973   *Widowhood in an American City.* Cambridge: Schenkman Pub-
        lishing Co.

Maddison, David
1968   "Relevance of Conjugal Bereavement for Preventive Psychiatry."
        British Journal of Medical Psychology 41: 223–233.

Mayer, John E. and Noel Timms
1970   *The Client Speaks.* New York: Atherton Press.

Metropolitan Life Insurance Company
1962   "The American Widow." *Statistical Bulletin* 43 (Nov.): 1–4.

Parkes, C. Murray
1964   "Grief as an Illness." *New Society* (April).

1972   *Bereavement: Studies of Grief in Adult Life.* New York: Inter-
        national Press.

Shanas, Ethel
1968   *Old People in Three Industrial Societies.* New York: Atherton
        Press.

Silverman, Phyllis R.
1966   "Services for the Widowed during the Period of Bereavement,"
        in *Social Work Practices.* New York: Columbia University Press,
        pp. 170–189.

1969   "The Widow-to-Widow Program: An Experiment in Preventive
        Intervention." *Mental Hygiene* 53: 333–337.

1970   "The Widow as a Caregiver in a Program of Preventive Intervention
        with Other Widows." *Mental Hygiene* 54: 540–547.

1972   "Widowhood and Preventive Intervention." *The Family Coordina-
        tor* 21: 95-1-2.

VanCoevering, Virginia
1971   "Developmental Tasks of Widowhood for the Aging Woman."
        Paper presented at the 1971 meeting of the American Psychological
        Association.

Weiss, Carol
1972A   *Evaluation Research: Methods of Assessing Program Effective-
        ness.* Englewood Cliffs: Prentice-Hall Inc.
1972B   *Evaluating Action Programs: Readings in Social Action and
        Education.* Boston: Allyn and Bacon, Inc.

Weiss, Robert S.
1974   *Loneliness: The Experience of Emotional and Social Isolation.*
        Cambridge: The M. I. T. Press.
1975   "Transition States and Other Stressful Situations: Their Nature
        and Programs for Their Management," to appear in Caplan and
        Killilea (eds.), *Support Systems and Mutual Help.* Forthcoming
        1976.

Weiss, Robert S. and Martin Rein
1971   "The Evaluation of Broad-Aim Programs: A Cautionary Case
        and a Moral," in Caro (ed.), *Readings in Evaluation Research.*
        New York: Russell Sage Foundation.

INDEX